CYCLE C

CELEBRATIONS OF THE WORD FOR CHILDREN

CYCLE C

CELEBRATIONS

OF THE

WORD

FOR CHILDREN

WRITTEN BY BERNICE STADLER

EDITED BY NANCY REECE

TWENTY-THIRD PUBLICATIONS

Mystic, Connecticut

To all parish volunteers who contribute to children's worship.

For the hours given at meetings coordinating and evaluating; for your endless cutting, gluing, painting, hammering, and sewing.

Because of your generosity, saying yes to the Lord, something beautiful is being made for our children, for our God.

Twenty-Third Publications
P.O. Box 180
Mystic, CT 06355
(203) 536-2611

Library of Congress Catalog Card Number 88-90102
ISBN 0-89622-362-0

CONTENTS

INTRODUCTION

The word of God that we hear each Sunday should be truly good news—to guide us, strengthen us, comfort us. But do our children agree? During the Eucharist, or even during instruction at home or in the classroom, do children experience the good news of Scripture and the lesson? We feared not. We feared that, for the most part in a typical adult-oriented service, the children have "tuned out." Perhaps the ideas presented are too sophisticated, wordy, or don't apply to the child's life. Or the presentation is so standard a child is tempted to daydream through it.

Our concern that children were not really part of our worship rituals culminated six years ago in the formation of the Children's Liturgy Committee in our church. With families with younger children in mind, the committee began planning once-a-month Masses directed at and including such families in the service. Because members of the committee wanted our children to appreciate and understand God's word, the Masses were designed to use children in many roles: as Scripture readers, as song leaders, as actors in dramatic presentations of the gospels, and as participants in the homily discussion.

Since its formation, the committee has met dozens of times sharing ideas, brainstorming, and creating services that focus on children's understanding of the teachings of the church. The response to these celebrations has been excellent. Every two or three years we survey the congregation attending the children's liturgies (approximately 500 adults and children) to see if this style of liturgy is still appreciated and desired. So far so good!

Although created in a liturgical setting, the 18 celebrations contained in this book are not designed to be used in one setting exclusively. They may be used in a classroom situation, or when instruction takes place in a private home, or they can be adapted for use in a liturgical setting. Our hope is that, however used, these celebrations will make religious ritual more accessible to children.

Glancing through the services, the reader will notice that the lessons are prepared in detail for an adult Presenter, with cues for the Presenter's motions and responses of the children. In our experience, Presenters appreciate knowing what is expected of them, what is the message or attitude to be developed with the children, and "What am I to do with this prop?" If presiding adults are not comfortable with what is planned, they can make changes that are compatible with their personalities.

To liven up the celebration, remembering it is for children, we use a variety of lesson methods. One of our favorites is storytelling. Doesn't everyone love a story? Using an opaque projector (our public schools allow us to use theirs) we enlarge the pictures in the children's literature book we are using, cut them out of poster board, and color them with bright paints or markers. Tape roles are adhered to the back sides. The pictures are placed on the floor around our large easel (a parishioner made one to hold a 4' x 6' flannel-covered board). Two prepared students put up and take down the appropriate pictures while the Presenter narrates the story. We also use transparencies of pictures with an overhead projector and screen while the story is narrated. The results, judging from the children's response, are worth our efforts.

Filmstrips (no longer than six minutes), puppets used by a Presenter who is a bit of an actor, props, actors "walking on" to help with the lesson—all of these create an activity children respond to. Other patterns in the celebrations—repeating aloud of Scripture names or learning sign language for a particular phrase—imprint the message of the lesson on the children's minds and hearts. After the lesson, hand-outs create a visual reminder of the gospel message. In our routine, supplies for making props and hand-outs are given to the committee members at least a month before the celebration.

In our community, after the scripts are typed, the committee chairperson and the member in charge for that specific service meet with the Presenter. They talk through the service, demonstrating sign language or motions with props. Last minute changes are made and reported back to the committee. Every committee member has a copy of the script and is expected to know who is in charge of details like lights, cueing actors, music, filmstrips, passing hand-outs, etc. In the case of liturgical use, scripts are also given to the organist and adult cantors two weeks before the service.

The list of scriptural readings in each section identifies this particular Sunday in Cycle C. Since these celebrations are not strictly intended for use at Sunday Eucharist, all three readings are not included in the service. In some of the services, the gospel reading is rewritten as a dramatization or narration. In others, the Presenter simply reads the gospel from a Bible. To shorten the service because it is for children, we prefer including just the First Reading and the gospel. In our experience, we have learned to choose older children (sixth grade and older) as Readers, Prayer Leaders, and speaking actors, and children in fifth grade and above in the non-speaking roles. We realize that many younger children would love to speak parts or lead a prayer, and their mothers would love it, but for the most part working with older children produces smoother practices and more meaningful services. The younger children, then, look forward to their own participation.

In our parish, at the beginning of each celebration, children pass out song sheets with words to all the songs we will be singing, and programs with responses to the prayers. We try to keep the commotion down, setting a mood of reverence by playing recorded music we will use again during the service. We do not practice songs before the service—feeling that's like having a dry run of "Happy Birthday" in front of the birthday child! But in this and other ways, the celebrations are flexible, adaptable to particular situations and preferences. To encourage all the children to participate, we suggest two songs in each service, indicating sources in parentheses after the song title. Our suggestions, of course, can be replaced with other favorites. For our part, we have included music we know children like, not always liturgical in nature, but cheerful, upbeat songs that are easy to learn.

The abbreviations identifying sources for particular songs refer to *Hi God II* and *III*, *Bloom Where You Are Planted (BWYAP)*, and *Color the World With Song (CTWWS)*. All three are albums by Carey Landry available from North American Liturgical Resources (NALR), 10802 N. 23rd Avenue, Phoenix, AZ 95209.

In our parish these children-oriented services, whether presented in church, in a classroom or in a home answer in part our concern that children are "tuning out" during adult-directed services. We hope these 18 celebrations will answer similar needs in other parishes and will inspire more creative efforts on behalf of and by children.

"THE CROOKED SHALL
BE MADE STRAIGHT"

(SECOND SUNDAY OF ADVENT—Winter)

Baruch 5:1-9   Philippians 1:4-6,8-11   Luke 3:1-6

THEME
Shape up joyfully! The Kingdom of God is at hand

PROPS
1. Words on a back wall: "The Crooked Shall Be Made Straight"

2. On the back wall is a paper house with a crooked house number sign, a crooked mailbox, a city sign, "Bent Town," that is bent, some bushes. All the signs are to be adjusted later. A free-standing lamp post (a six-foot 2"x4" on a stand with a cardboard lamp). The arm holding the lamp is crooked.

3. An older student plays the part of John the Baptist in the gospel. His costume is a burlap tunic, a fur chest-piece and a walking stick.

4. In the lesson, the play "The Crooked Town" by Gordon C. Bennett is read by 3 students and pantomimed by 4-5 students. A cart to hold peddler's goods, a full length mirror, and kazoos are also needed.

5. Kazoos, purchased or home-made (5" posterboard rolls with a waxed paper piece attached with a rubber band at one end). On the rolls is imprinted, "Prepare His Way With a Joyful Heart!"

PERSONNEL
1. Presenter
2. Song Leader
3. Prayer Leader
4. Reader
5. Older student: John the Baptist
6. 3 older students for readers.
7. 4-5 students as pantomime townsfolk and peddler

GREETING

PRESENTER   Welcome, my brothers and sisters, on this Second Sunday of Advent. During this holy season the church calls out "Marana-tha" (mah-<u>rah</u>-nah-tha). Say that with me, Maranatha. It means "Come, Lord Jesus." Let's call that again with sign laguage.

(Signs for "Come, Lord Jesus" are:
Come: hands out, palms up
Lord: right hand makes an L shape with index and thumb, sweep down across chest from left shoulder to right waist
Jesus: right index touches the palm of the left hand, and then the left index touches the palm of the right hand.)

PRESENTER   Maranatha, come, Lord Jesus!

OPENING PRAYER

PRAYER LEADER   Heavenly Father, you call us here to anticipate the coming of your son, Jesus, into our lives. Help us prepare loving homes for him in our hearts. Amen.

FIRST READING

READER   Baruch 5:1-9

SONG LEADER   "Make A Joyful Noise" (*CTWWS*)

GOSPEL

PRESENTER   In the fifteenth year of the rule of Tiberius Caesar, when Pontius Pilate was procurator of Judea, when Herold was tetrarch of Galilee, during the high priesthood of Annas and Caiaphas, the word of God was spoken to John, son of Zechariah, in the desert.

(John the Baptist walks out into the center worship space. He is dressed in a burlap tunic with a fur skin across his chest. He is barefooted and carries a large walking stick.)

PRESENTER   John went about the entire region of the Jordan proclaiming a baptism of repentance which led to the forgiveness of sins.

(John walks down the center aisle, lifting his stick raising his other hand saying...)

JOHN Repent! I say, change your ways! The Kingdom of God is at hand! Prepare his way! Turn your hearts to him!

(Repeat these acclamations if necessary, and then leave the room.)

PRESENTER John did as is written in the book of Isaiah the prophet: "A herald's voice in the desert, crying, 'Make ready the way of the Lord, clear him a straight path. Every valley shall be filled and every mountain and hill shall be leveled. The crooked roads shall be made straight and the rough ways smooth, and all mankind shall see the salvation of God.' " This is the gospel of the Lord.

LESSON

PRESENTER In our gospel there appears an important Advent character, John the Baptist. What was his message? Did you hear what he was calling out to the people of God? ("Repent! Change your ways! Prepare the way! Turn your hearts to God!") John was getting the people ready for Jesus. He was shaping them up! The gospel also said the "crooked roads shall be made straight." I know a story about people who received a similar message. Let's look and listen.

("THE CROOKED TOWN" by Gordon C. Bennett. Three older students are Voices 1, 2 and 3 standing at 3 different microphones, right, left and center stage. 4-5 other students pantomime townsfolk and peddler. In the peddler's cart are the items for sale: a full-length mirror, and kazoos in a bag.)

THE CROOKED TOWN

VOICE 1 We all know the rhyme about the crooked man who lived in a crooked house, but there was once a whole town, believe it or not, that was crooked. It was called Bent Town and it was where all the Bent People lived. They say it happened because an evil witch once put a curse on the place. At any rate, Bent Town was the oddest place you ever saw.

VOICE 2	Everything was crooked.
VOICE 3	The streets were crooked,
VOICE 1	the calendar was crooked,
VOICE 2	and the government was crooked.
VOICE 3	Which of course, means that the people were crooked. They looked very bony, for their arms and legs stuck out at strange angles,
	(The townsfolk enter, bent over, arms held at angles.)
VOICE 1	their backs were twisted and misshapen,
VOICE 2	and their faces were bent into perpetual scowls.
VOICE 3	They walked funny, zigzagging and bumping into each other. And their ways were mean and devious. Any man or woman would, without provocation, stomp and steal *(Show pickpocketing and teasing actions.)*
VOICE 1	or slander and slobber,
VOICE 2	or shun, shiver, and shame
VOICE 3	his wife or husband, neighbor, or fellow citizen.
VOICE 1	Conversation in Bent Town was devious and indirect. If you said, "Good morning," somebody might reply,
VOICE 2	"Is it?"
VOICE 1	or...
VOICE 2	"You don't say."
VOICE 1	And if you asked, "What time is it?" a person might answer,
VOICE 3	"Time to look out for yourself, pal, heh-heh.
VOICE 1	That was the best you could expect. The worst would be some sort of insult like

VOICE 3   "It's time to fix your face, ugly,"

VOICE 1   or...

VOICE 3   "It's way past your bedtime, dummy."

(During these "greetings" the townsfolk remain in one spot. They will change their body position when they answer.)

VOICE 1   or worse.... Such was life in Bent Town. Sinister, sad, morose, and melancholy.... Until the Peddler came.

(The Peddler enters with his cart.)

VOICE 2   No one had ever seen the Peddler before, and since the town seldom had visitors (for obvious reasons), he was a curiosity. The Peddler was a portly fellow with a red flannel shirt and a way of smiling all over his body. He walked beside a cart pulled by a donkey. Suddenly one morning, the donkey, the cart, and the Peddler appeared in the twisted alleys of Bent Town and pulled to a stop in the skewed square that passed for a marketplace.

VOICE 3   "Trinkets for sale! Ho-ho!"

VOICE 2   called the Peddler.

VOICE 3   "Trinkets for sale!"

VOICE 2   Nobody bought anything, for that was not the way in Bent Town. Everyone simply took what he wanted.

(The townsfolk remove the articles from the cart.)

VOICE 2   Soon the Peddler's cart was empty except for a brown bag and a gray canvas that stretched over the floor. The Peddler, still smiling, turned to the assembled bent multitude.

VOICE 3   "Dear friends, you have taken all that I have. That is, all that I have except for two items which have been designed to improve your...ah...your disposition!"

VOICE 2   And he removed the canvas from the floor of the cart, uncovering the first item and holding it up for them to see.

(Peddler takes out the mirror.)

VOICE 1   It was a full-length mirror.

(Each townsfolk sees himself in the mirror.)

VOICE 2   Now the witch had broken all of their mirrors, long ago, before these people were born. So, for the first time, everyone could see himself and realize that he, as well as his neighbors, was crooked. Very upsetting indeed!

VOICE 1   So each person asked a fellow townsmen to straighten him out. Which they did. You never heard such a rending...

VOICE 2   and cracking...

VOICE 1   and bending...

VOICE 2   and racking...

(Townsfolk helping each other straighten up.)

VOICE 1   ...in all your life. And when they had finished with each other, they set about transforming the town. Everything was straightened, from the judge's bench to the street-corner lamp-posts.

VOICE 2   The people walked straight and tall and from henceforth spoke the truth. But they were still sad.

(The townsfolk should emphasize gloomy faces.)

VOICE 1   The reason being that everyone was feeling guilty for the past.

VOICE 3   "It's all right!"

VOICE 1   cried the Peddler.

VOICE 3   "Past is preparation. Live and forget. Forget and live!"

VOICE 2   And he took his brown bag out of his cart, and he took a funny little thing out of his brown bag, and he put the funny little thing to his mouth. It was a kazoo.

(Peddler plays a note on the kazoo.)

VOICE 2   He played a gay tune, and the people were enchanted,

(The Peddler gives a kazoo to Voice 2 and 3.)

VOICE 1   for long ago, the witch had taken their musical instruments.

(Voices 2 and 3 play a tune under the rest of the speech, keeping the speech strong. Suggestion: "Lord of the Dance.")

VOICE 1   So the Peddler passed out kazoos all over town, and everyone made merry until two o'clock in the morning. The town rang with shrieks of laughter and the beat of dancing feet. And the witch's spell was broken.

(Everyone is playing on kazoos. Let the tune end before Voice 3 continues.)

VOICE 3   The Peddler was gone the next day and no one is sure what happened to him. Rumor has it that he was drowned in a river by the angry witch whose spell was broken. Others claim that he appeared in several other towns years later. But one thing's certain—Bent Town was never the same again. Life there goes on very differently since his visit.

VOICE 2   It is is not a paradise, it is at least closer than we know. *(pause)*

VOICE 1   So ... think carefully.... What is the task of the people of God this Advent?

VOICE 2   To hold up mirrors?

VOICE 3   To pass out kazoos? *(pause)*

ALL   *(with a uniform gesture)* Right!

PRESENTER   Thank you for sharing your two Advent messages. Yes, we will look into our mirrors this Advent. We will look with God's eyes to see what needs to be straightened in our lives. Perhaps we need to be kinder, or not complain so much. Perhaps we need to be more obedient, or to take more time for prayer.

And while we are straightening we will spread a joyful attitude among one another, not with fake grins and false cheerfulness, but with the deep joy and hope that God's Son brings. In our hearts we will play the peddler's kazoo.

The townsfolk will now give each of the children a kazoo to remind them of their story. Let's get into practice by playing one verse of "I've Got That Joy, Joy" (*Hi God I*), or "Thank You, Lord" (*Hi God I*) or any peppy song that the kids are familiar with.)

(*The children are sent back to their seats after the lesson.*)

COMMUNAL PRAYER

PRAYER LEADER   Please respond: "Come and be born in our hearts."

Lord, help us look truthfully at ourselves so that we may walk in your right path, we pray ... Come and be born in our hearts.

Lord, show us those people in our neighborhood and church that need a sign of our caring during this Christmas time, we pray ... Come and be born in our hearts.

Lord, we pray that your Holy Spirit touches with joy the hearts of those children who experience pain from sickness, or family problems, we pray ... Come and be born in our hearts.

SONG LEADER   "A Wondrous Work of Art" (*Hi God III*)

OUR HEARTS RING WITH PEACE, HOPE AND JOY

(CHRISTMAS EVE—Winter)

Isaiah 62:1-5 Matthew 1:1-25

PROPS

1. 8-10 plastic crate cubes covered with white fabric or paper, for shepherd's seats.

2. 8-10 shepherd staffs (1"x1/2"x4' wooden poles). 3"-4" long sections can be cut and nailed perpendicular onto the top of the staff. A bell is to be tied to this portion.

3. 6 narrow double-faced banners are carried in the entrance procession and used in the lesson. 6 blue sides and 6 red sides. All 1' wide, 2 are 3 1/2' long, 2 are 3' long, 2 are 2 1/2'. All the banners have a chevron point at the bottom. The blue banners have white stars. The red banners have the word "Joy" on 2 short pieces, "Hope" on 2 medium pieces and "Peace" on the 2 long pieces. Brass bells are tied on to the top and point portions of the red banners.

4. 4 large bells of different types: sleigh bell, brass bell, glass bell, crockery bell are used in the lesson.

5. A xylophone is used for beginning comments and the lesson.

6. Small jingle bells: 2-3 (or 1 small brass bell) tied onto a ribbon or piece of yarn for each participant. You could also attach a tag that says, "My heart rings with Peace, Hope, Joy—Christmas 19___."

7. Baby doll and a manger

PARTICIPANTS

1. Presenter
2. Prayer Leader
3. Reader
4. Song Leader
5. Gospel actors: 10 Angels, 8-10 Shepherds, Mary, Joseph, and Lead Angel.

GREETING

(Flute and xylophone play the first 3 lines of "Choral of the Bells." The xylophone then chimes 3 times simulating a clock.)

SONG LEADER   The waiting is over! (*chimes struck*) Christmas has come. (*chimes struck*)
Don your dress of celebration! (*chimes struck*) The Savior is born!
Let us stand and sing "Joy to the World."

ENTRANCE PROCESSION

(6 Bell banners, 10 Shepherd, 10 Angels, Mary, Joseph, Lead Angel, Reader, Presenter.)

(The shepherds and the angels walk right up into the worship area. The shepherds sit and the Angels stand behind them.)

GREETING

PRESENTER   Merry Christmas to you all. How happy we are, the shepherds, the angels, and all of us here to be gathered on this Holy Night, the night of our Savior's birth. As we begin this celebration, let us sing our praises to God with the song the angels began almost 2000 years ago. Our own angels here will lead us in the motions.

SONG LEADER   "Glory Be" (*BWYAP*)

(The shepherds ring their staff bells for the words "Glory be" only. The angels show motions during the refrain.)

Angel motions:
Glory be: Begin with hands together, palms touching. Raise both hands together above head, then separate them, spreading them out and down into large circles.

To the Father: Bring hands together, chest high, palms facing up.

To the Son: Touch middle finger of right hand to palm of the left hand. Then touch the middle finger of the left hand to the palm of the right hand. To the Spirit: Cross arms over chest. All Glory to Our God: same motion as "Glory Be"; then return hands to starting position.)

FIRST READING

READER   Isaiah 62:1-5

GOSPEL

PRESENTER   It's time for our wonderful story to be told. Would the children like to come up and sit on the floor? If any of the children are 3 or under we ask that a Mom or Dad come up with them.

READER   (*Waits until everyone is settled.*) A reading according to the gospel of St. Luke.
In those days Caesar Augustus published a decree ordering a census be taken of the whole Roman world. Everyone went to register, each to his own town.

(Mary and Joseph begin walking.)

And so Joseph went from the town of Nazareth in Galilee to Judea into David's town of Bethlehem because he was of the same line as David. He went to register with Mary, his promised wife, who was with child.

(Mary and Joseph walk into the worship area, kneel and place the baby in the manger. All angels kneel.)

While they were there the time came for Mary to have her child. She gave birth to her first-born son, wrapped him in swaddling clothes and laid him in a manger, because there was no room for them at the inn.

(An angel comes forward, picks up the baby, and sings while rocking the baby [Braham's Lullaby melody]):

Hush-a-by, don't you cry
Oh sweet Baby Jesus,
Mother dear will hold you near,
All thru the night!

SONG LEADER (*Leads the congregation in repeating this song while the angel returns the baby to the manger.*)

PRESENTER   There were shepherds in the countryside, living in the fields and keeping night watch over their flocks.

The angel of the Lord appeared to them, as the glory of the Lord shone around them.

(The lead angel steps in front of the manger, holding her arms out to the shepherds. The shepherds cover their eyes with their left arms.)

PRESENTER   The shepherds were very much afraid.
The angel said to them:

(During these lines an angel uses dramatic motions.)

"You have nothing to fear! (*gives sign for peace: hands form "teepee," then draw out and down*) I come to proclaim good news to you (*arms above head clapping once*), tidings of great joy to be shared by the whole people. This day in David's city, (*bows*) a Savior has been born to you, the Messiah and Lord! (*right arm above head*) Let this be a sign to you.

(*rocking arms*) You will find the infant wrapped in swaddling clothes and lying in a manger.

Suddenly, there was with the angel a multitude of the heavenly host, praising God and singing:

(Small angels stand, join hands and raise their arms. Shepherds ring their bells.)

SONG LEADER   *(leads the congregation in singing "Gloria in Excelsis Deo"—tune from refrain of "Angels We Have Heard on High")*

"Gloria in Excelsis Deo,
Gloria in Excelsis Deo."

The shepherds went quickly into Bethlehem and found the baby lying in the manger. Once they saw they understood what the angels told them. They returned glorifying and praising God for all they had seen and heard.
This is the Good News of the Lord!

SONG LEADER   Leads congregation in "Gloria in Excelsis Deo." (*Shepherd's bells ring.*)

LESSON

PRESENTER   Did you notice the bells on all the shepherd's staffs? They sounded pretty, didn't they? We see and hear a lot of bells at Christmas time. I see them on the wreath's of your front doors, on Christmas cards, on the ornaments on the tree. Did any of you make some bells at school? We have some special bells here.

(At this time 4 children will come up, each holding a different style bell. Have them ring their bell and comment on the different tones.)

All of these bells are different with a ring of its own. Let's imagine that these bells had voices. If they could speak on this Christmas Eve, the birth of the Lord Jesus, what would they say? What would be their message? *(response)* Yes, I agree with you, all these messages and especially they would ring out.

(Go to sky banners and turn each of the six around exposing the reverse sides with the words Peace, Hope, Joy, Peace, Hope, Joy.)

Peace, Hope, and Joy: the gifts that Jesus brought to us when he was born.

Did you know that each of us has a bell deep down inside of us? Yes, we do. You may say, "I've never heard it." Believe me, it's there. Perhaps you've never shaken it.

Each of our bells is different, just like these *(motioning to those the four children are holding)*. Some of ours are loud, some are soft and delicate. God our Father wants to hear our heart bells ringing with peace, hope, and joy. If we really believe in his Son, Jesus, that he came to set us free, we will spread this message to everyone we meet. Just by the way we act and smile and care for one another, others will be able to hear our bells ringing.

God our Father is listening to us and although he loves the sound that we each can make, he mostly loves the harmony we can make by ringing together.

Let me show you. _____ *(name)* would you show us how a high bell-message sounds. *(plays line "Joy to the world, the Lord in born" with one mallet).* And a low sound *(plays the same line in a lower tone).* And now in harmony *(line is repeated with 2 or 3 mallets).* Let's sing that line with _____ *(name).*

(All sing "Joy to the World, the Lord Is Born!")

So children, on this night and all this next year be sure to let your message ring! To remind you, we have a little bell for each of you. We'll see that you get it after this celebration is concluded.

COMMUNAL PRAYER

PRAYER LEADER   Let us respond, "Father of Jesus, hear our prayer."

We ask for peace in our world, especially for our brothers and sisters in the Middle East, South Africa, Ireland, Central America, the Philippines and Haiti, we pray to the Lord.... Father of Jesus, hear our prayer.

We ask the Holy Spirit to give us courage to spread the message that Jesus brought to earth, we pray to the Lord... Father of Jesus, hear our prayer.

We give thanks for the gift of our families and friends. Lord help us become friends of the lonely, we pray to the Lord... Father of Jesus, hear our prayer.

SONG LEADER   Leads congregation in "Hark the Herald Angels Sing"

HAPPY BIRTHDAY, BABY JESUS

(CHRISTMAS EVE—Winter)

Isaiah 62:1-5 Matthew 1:1-25

THEME   A birthday party for Jesus

PROPS   1. Very large birthday cake with candles.(We prepared and froze ten 13"x9" sheet cakes weeks before the event. Two days before the celebration the cake was layered into a 3-tiered form, iced, decorated with at least 50 candles. A sponge cake recipe is good because of its solid texture.) The cake is placed on a serving cart and brought up in the entrance procession.

2. A large (3'x4' cardboard) free-standing birthday card is placed near the entrance with an older child or an adult greeter inviting the children to sign the card. (Use an opaque projector to copy a purchased card or have the children draw the design) This card is brought up in the entrance procession.

3. Three sections of gospel scenery: (4'x 6' cardboard pieces supported by wooden feet), "Hotel Bethlehem" stable (placed a few feet further back), hillside with star-filled sky next to the stable scene. (Use opaque projector to save time drawing these scenes.)

4. Sound-effect instruments for gospel participation:
   A. Kazoos: Toilet tissue rolls with a piece of waxed paper fastened with rubber band at one end
   B. 2-3 jingle bells tied onto yarn or ribbon (several sets)
   C. Knockers: 2 small pieces of wood (several sets)
   D. Megaphones: posterboard piece rolled into cone shapes. On sides of megaphones is printed one of these sayings: "Cows for sale!" "Get your olives here" "Buy a good sheep!" "Moo-oo-oo," "Baa-aa-aa," "Cluck, Cluck."

5. Baskets or boxes to collect instruments

6. Large gift-wrapped box with removable lid and several pre-cut posterboard (paper covered styrofoam or plywood is more of a visual), shapes of a heart, face, feet, hand, (about 10"-12" square) to be used in lesson

7. If an altar is used, decorate with crepe paper and place several helium balloons around the altar.

PERSONNEL   1. Presenter

2. Prayer Leader

3. Reader

4. Song Leader

5. Gospel Actors: Messenger, Mary, Joseph, Angel Hotel Keeper, Two or Three Shepherds

6. Two children to carry card

7. Adult to bring in the cake at the entrance procession

8. Greeter

9. Several adults to lead children with sound effects during practice and gospel telling

(Before the celebration begins, all children should come up and sit on the floor. The floor is marked in the following sections: 1) Messengers, 2) Bells, 3) Door knockers, 4) Animals, 5) Vendors. One adult leader should be with each group. They remain with their section to help with the gospel telling. The presenter should have a very short practice with the sound effects. Ask them to keep the noisemakers quiet until it is their turn to participate.)

GREETING

Merry Christmas to you all, and a happy birthday to Jesus! Today we're having a special birthday party. Let's stand and sing "Happy Birthday" to Jesus while _____(Name of presenter) enters with a special sign of this party.

(Entrance procession: adult with birthday cake an lit candles, children with birthday card, and the presenter)

SONG LEADER   *(Leads congregation in singing "Happy Birthday")*

Merry Christmas and welcome to Jesus' birthday celebration! Before we blow out the candles, let us all first close our eyes and make a big wish. Okay, Ready? *(Choose 4 or 5 children to help blow out the candles.)*

This is some cake! All of the children will get a piece of the cake after our celebration. *(Cake is then removed by a helper to be sliced in another room.)* And what a beautiful greeting card. Let's put the card over here so we can all see it.

Do you know why we send birthday cards and celebrate with birthday parties? I think it's to say to that person, "We're happy that you were born. We're happy that you are here with us now!" That's why I think we celebrate birthdays.

Tonight we say to Jesus, "Jesus, how happy we are to be here! We're so glad that you were born. We're glad that you're here to give us all your love."

FIRST READING

Isaiah 62:1-5
"Come, Lord Jesus" (*Hi God II*) (*Use hand motions.*)

GOSPEL

PRESENTER   We will not only listen to God's Word, but you children will help tell the story with your instruments.

(*Invite all adults to be seated.*)

CHRISTMAS NARRATIVE

PRESENTER   About 2000 years ago, in the town of Nazareth, where Mary and Joseph lived, a messenger from Emperor Caesar Augustus road into town.

SOUND 1   (Kazoos: *trumpeting sound, done twice*)

MESSENGER   "Hear ye, Hear ye! Everyone in this part of the country must go to his home town to register. The Emperor wants a census to be taken!"

(*At this time Mary and Joseph start slowly toward the front from halfway down an aisle.*)

PRESENTER   So Mary and Joseph, obedient citizens, left the next day on their trip to Bethlehem because that was Joseph's home town. Mary was pregnant. It was almost time for her baby to be born, so she rode on their donkey and Joseph walked. It was a long, tiresome journey, and during the nights all you could hear was the slow, steady ringing of the donkey's bells.

SOUND 2   Jingle bells: ring, ring, ring. (*slow beat*)

SONG LEADER	(leads congregation) "Silent night, holy night, All is calm, all is bright."
	(Mary and Joseph now at the front of the worship space.)
PRESENTER	When Mary and Joseph finally reached Bethlehem, it was late afternoon and the city was crowded and very busy with vendors, selling their fruits and animals, people bargaining and buying. Such a clamor!
SOUND 3	(Animals and vendors call out what is written on their megaphones.)
	(Mary and Joseph walk slowly toward the hotel.)
PRESENTER	(Give sign for the "town" to quiet down) Joseph started to look for a place for them to stay right away. Since it was late and the city so crowded, his chances to find a night's lodging were not good. He knocked on hotel doors...
SOUND 4	Door knockers: knock, knock, knock.
PRESENTER	And knocked...
SOUND 4	Door knockers: knock, knock, knock
PRESENTER	And knocked...
SOUND 4	Door knockers: knock, knock, knock
PRESENTER	Finally a hotel keeper said:
HOTEL KEEPER	"You can use my stable in back for the night if you want."
	(Mary and Joseph go to the stable and sit on floor. Baby Jesus is in a crib in the stable.)
PRESENTER	So Mary and Joseph took him up on his offer. The stable was filled with animals: a cow, sheep, and chickens. They helped to keep the stable warm.
SOUND 5	Animals: mooing, baaing, cluck-clucking.

PRESENTER	Joseph found some clean straw and made a place for Mary to rest. During that night, Mary gave birth to her son and wrapped him in swaddling clothes and kept him close to her.
SONG LEADER	(*Leads congregation in entire first verse of "Silent Night." During the singing, shepherds gather in front of the hill scene.*)
PRESENTER	In the neighborhood there were shepherds on the hills, guarding their flocks of sheep. The shepherds were talking among themselves. Suddenly a musical sound filled the air.
SOUND 6	Bells (*fast shaking*) (*Angel walks to where the shepherds are standing*)
PRESENTER	An angel appeared before them. The shepherds were scared but the angel said:
ANGEL	"Don't be afraid."
PRESENTER	I bring you great news! Today a savior has been born to you! He is Christ the Lord. You will find the baby wrapped in swaddling clothes and lying in a manger. And suddenly the whole sky was filled with a choir of angels...
SOUND 6	Bells (*fast shaking*)
PRESENTER	(*Singing "Glory to God in the highest and peace to men of good will"*) The shepherds went and found the baby, glorifying and praising God for all that they had heard and seen. This is the very good news of the Lord.
SONG LEADER	"Gloria in Excelsis Deo" (*Refrain from "Angels We Have Heard on High"*)

LESSON

PRESENTER	That was a beautiful story that we all took part in! Thanks to all the actors and sound makers. Let's hear it from the kazoos once more (*wait for noise*), now the bells (*wait*), the door knockers (*wait*), the animals and vendors (*wait*). What a joyous noise for this birthday party. Now let's put our instru-

ments in the baskets so that we can talk about something special (*wait*).

Tonight is an exciting night, isn't it? Why are you excited? (*get some responses: Santa's coming, getting gifts, giving gifts*) It's fun opening presents, isn't it? Did some of you buy or make your Moms and Dads or sisters or brothers a gift? (*ask for hands*) Sh-h-h-h, don't tell what it is. It's a secret, right?

Do you bring birthday presents to a boy or girl at their birthday party? (*wait for response*) Well, tonight is Jesus' birthday party. What kind of gift can we give him? Lets think about that for a moment. (*get gift-wrapped box*) I have a gift box here, but it's empty. What can we put into it?

Does Jesus need toys like dolls, games or racing cars? (*no*) If he doesn't want things like that, what would he like from us?

(When a child offers a suggestion for a gift such as love, prayers, kind acts, feeding the hungry , doing chores at home, studying well in school, being cheerful, obeying parents etc, comment that that's a fine gift to give and that you happen to have a symbol appropriate for that gift. You will then write the name of the action or virtue onto the paper [or styrofoam or wooden shape such as heart, face, foot, or hand.] Ask how many want to give that gift, and then write and comment, "About 20 of us are giving this gift of chores," or "All of us are giving this one, "etc. After you have put several symbols in the gift box continue:)

PRESENTER

I'm sure Jesus will like our gifts to him. Let us put on the lid and top it off with a bow. How will we give this gift to him? Where is he? (The children may say that he's in the manger as a baby.) Is he here with us? Yes! Jesus said that whenever we get together to talk about him and pray to him, he'll be there. So let's sit with our hands in our laps with the palms facing up, like this (*demonstrate*), close our eyes and wait a moment while Jesus looks upon our gift. (*pause*) Now repeat this prayer after me. Dear Lord Jesus, (*repeat*) we love you, (*repeat*) receive these gifts from your children (*repeat*) Amen. (*repeat*)

I'll put this package over here, near the crib. Now let's all sing happy birthday to Jesus once more and then you can return to your seats.

SONG LEADER   "Happy Birthday"

COMMUNAL PRAYER

PRAYER LEADER   Now it's time to ask God to help us in our need. To each of our petitions, we will answer,"Come to us, Jesus."

For our families, that we may be thankful for each other we pray... Come to us, Jesus.

For all the countries of the world, that wars may end and peace begin, we pray ... Come to us, Jesus.

For our pastor and our teachers, we thank God for their gifts to us. May they continue to lead us to the Lord, we pray ... Come to us, Jesus.

SONG LEADER   Slices of Jesus' birthday cake will be given to all children at the close of our celebration.

(Leads everyone in singing "We Wish You a Merry Christ mas," or "Joy to the World.")

FILLED WITH GOD'S BLESSINGS

(BAPTISM OF THE LORD—Winter)

Isaiah 42:1-4,6-7 Acts 10:34-38 Luke 3:15-16,21-22

THEME   By our baptismal waters we are filled with the Spirit of God. We will experience this if we believe.

PROPS

1. The worship space where the children will sit is masked off in a horseshoe fashion. Two rows may be needed. A small table is set up in the center of the horseshoe.
2. A baptismal font and a large scallop or clam shell is to be placed in the sanctuary.
3. A basket of laundry, a glass pitcher with a package of lemonade mix inside, and a dead-looking plant are to be brought in during the entrance procession and put on the small table in the sanctuary.
4. Two glass pitchers of water will be carried in during the entrance procession. This water is to be poured into the baptismal font.
5. A small scallop or clam shell is given to each child after the lesson. (Ask a seafood restaurant to save some cherrystone clam shells. Wash them in bleach water and then dry.) Inside the shell is glued a "water drop" shape paper typed with "Filled with God's Spirit."
6. The Presenter needs to know the sign language for: "Thank You," "Filled," and "Blessings."

PERSONNEL

1. Presenter
2. Song Leader
3. Prayer Leader
4. Reader
5. Children to bring up props during entrance procession
6. Adult to help bless the children during the lesson
7. Optional. An infant could be baptized during the celebration. If this option is chosen, the shells given to the children could have the name of the child baptized typed on the "water drop."

GREETING

PRESENTER   Good morning. Welcome to all of our family and friends. Today we celebrate the Spirit of God living within us. We are reminded of God's changing grace in us through our baptism.

OPENING PRAYER

PRAYER LEADER   Let us free ourselves now of any hard feelings we may have brought here today. Lord Jesus, help us to know ourselves, our strengths, and our weaknesses. Help us to always hear your message as you share with us your life and your love. Amen.

FIRST READING

READER   Isaiah 42:1-4, 6-8

SONG LEADER   "All the Time" (*CTWWS*)

PRE-GOSPEL COMMENTS

PRESENTER   On the floor we have two lines marked off with masking tape. We would like the children to come up and sit on those lines. (*Wait for the children to be settled.*) Before I read our gospel, I want to talk a bit about the items that were brought up in the entrance procession.

What do we have here? (*Pick up basket of laundry with box of detergent.*) (*response*) Yes, laundry and soap. What's this? (*Raise the glass pitcher with the envelope of lemonade mix.*) (*response*) And look at this plant! (*Hold it up.*) It looks like it's in sad shape!

Now who can tell me what these all have in common? What do they all need? Water! Right. Detergent without water can't clean clothes. And if you're thirsty what good is dry lemonade mix? This plant shows us what all living things would look like without water. So water is pretty important, isn't it?

Listen to our gospel now. Something is going to happen to Jesus. It has to do with water.

GOSPEL

PRESENTER   Luke 3:15-16, 21-22

LESSON

PRESENTER   What happened to Jesus? (*response*) He was baptized by St. John. In the river, water was poured over Jesus. Many times a shell, like this one (*holding up shell*) was used to pour the water. Those baptismal waters were a sign of a change in life. Jesus was beginning the job he came to earth for, his Father's work. He was filled with his Father's blessing, so filled that his Father said, "This is my Son. I am pleased with him."

Everyone here who is baptized, raise your hand. (*checking over the congregation and then the children*) Yes, you too! Baptism waters were poured over our heads from a font like this (*motioning to the baptismal font*) and our lives were changed. Just as water changes a thirsty plant or washes clothes, the waters of baptism changed us and made us members of God's family. It filled us with God's blessings.

Do we feel like we're filled with God's blessings most of the time? (*response*) A lot of the time we can feel dry like the thirsty plant. When we forget about God's presence in us, it's like turning off the water faucet. We want to keep the water of baptism flowing! Every day we will thank God for God's power and guidance of us, as Jesus did. Then, as God's family, we can do the good work God wants of us. God will say to us, "These are my sons and daughters and I am pleased with them."

Let us say in sign language, "Thank you for filling us with your blessings." ("*Thank You*": *right hand fingers touch chin then arm draws out and upward in one motion. "Filling": left hand made into fist as if holding a bouquet of flowers. Rub right hand once across the top of left hand. "Blessings": with both hands in a fist, place the thumb nail of each hand near the mouth, palms facing each other. Move hands forward and outward opening your palms so they are facing down.*)

I am now going to bless this water in our baptismal font. After I do this we will have you children line up two by two and _____ will mark your foreheads with this water to remind you of your own baptism and the privilege of being a member of God's family. While you are doing this, I will sprinkle your family with the same water to remind them too. When the water is felt, bless yourselves with the prayer, "The Father, Son, and Holy Spirit fill me with blessings."

27

(Presenter blesses the children. After the children are blessed, they are given a small scallop or clam shell. The children then return to their seats.)

SONG LEADER   Sings "You Have Been Baptized in Christ" (*Carey Landry, NALR*). (You might wish to play the recording of this song. It can be found in the *Abba Father* album.)

COMMUNAL PRAYER

PRAYER LEADER   The response today will be, "Fill us with your blessing."

Lord, like you we have a job to do: to feed the hungry, console the sad, teach the unlearned. Help us to do our job well, we pray... Fill us with you blessing.

Lord, help us as a parish to support one another so we may all grow in faith, we pray ... Fill us with your blessing.

Lord, help us to be aware of your grace within us that through you we can do whatever the Father wants us to do., we pray ... Fill us with your blessing.

SONG LEADER   "We Are Children of the Light" (*Hi God II*). If a child has been baptized, sing "You are a New Creation." (*Hi God III*)

GOOD NEWS

(THIRD SUNDAY OF THE YEAR—Winter)

Nehemiah 8:2-4, 5-6, 8-10   1 Corinthians 12:12-14,27   Luke 4:14-21

THEME	Jesus is our joy
PROPS	1. A sign that says "Jesus is our Joy" is to be placed on a wall or an easel.
	2. A scroll for each child, on which is imprinted Isaiah's words from the gospel, "The Spirit of the Lord is upon me to ... a year of favor from the Lord."(*Print total passage*) These should be rolled up and sealed with a red heart. Pass these out to the children as they come in. Ask them not to open them until they are asked to.
	3. A large scroll with the same quote as #2, to be used for the gospel proclamation.
	4. "The Little Brute Family" by Russell Hoban, (available in any school or public library) is read by the presenter with pictures shown from the book or an overhead projector to accompany the story. (To make transparencies, permission must be obtained from the publisher by writing and giving the date that it will be used for your celebration.)
PERSONNEL	1. Presenter
	2. Song Leader
	3. Prayer Leader
	4. Reader
	5. Helper to operate overhead projector

GREETING

PRESENTER   Welcome to all of you, my brothers and sisters.
These scrolls in our hands are news from God—good news
that brings tidings of joy, as our Scriptures will soon tell us.

OPENING PRAYER

PRAYER LEADER   Lord, we have a fresh new year to begin. Inspire us to use each
day to its fullest and let us be thankful for each of our blessings.

God, our heavenly Father, as we hear your word today, may we keep it in our hearts as we go about our daily work and. help others to share in it. We give you thanks and praise through Your Son, Jesus Christ, forever and ever.

FIRST READING

READER Nehemiah 8:2-4, 5-6, 8-10

SONG LEADER "This is the Day" (*Hi God II*)

GOSPEL

PRESENTER Luke 4:14-21

(When you read the words "he unrolled the scroll..." unroll the large scroll and read from it the words of the prophet Isaiah. Reroll it and then proceed with the rest of the gospel.)

LESSON

PRESENTER *(Ask the children to bring their scrolls and to sit in the sanctuary. Wait until everyone is settled.)*

In today's gospel we heard Jesus telling us some very good news. He read it from a scroll like the ones you have. You may open them now.

Let's read together from your scrolls. If you can't read yet, just listen to the words.

"The Spirit of the Lord is upon me; he has anointed me. He has sent me to bring good news to the poor, set the captives free, to give sight to the blind and release to prisoners, to announce a year of favor from the Lord."

If we believe in Jesus and the wonderful work he came to do, this news should fill us with joy, shouldn't it? Let's ask ourselves, "Am I a joyful person?" *(pause)* Asking this reminds me of a story that I would like to read to you about the Brute family.

(At this time, the story, The Little Brute Family, is read while the picture transparencies are shown on the overhead projector.)

That good feeling that Baby Brute found changed the whole family, didn't it? Do you think we Christians have found a "good feeling" like that? Jesus' words, like those in your hands, are like the good feeling. They have the power to change us, to make us a joyful people. Many times we forget about this "gospel joy" and let ourselves get grumpy and complain. Does that happen in your house? Do you get grumpy and argue? (*Wait for a response.*)

Sure, problems will upset all of us at times, but deep down if we believe in Jesus, the joy and hope remains there.

I've got an idea! How about all of you here being like Baby Brute and bringing a reminder of this good feeling home in this scroll. When you see at times the "good feeling" is lost for awhile, when joy is needed, place this scroll on the dinner table for everyone to see. Then everyone in your family will think of the "good feeling" the true gospel joy, and see if it returns.

COMMUNAL PRAYER

PRAYER LEADER   Our response today is "Father, hear our prayer."

Father, let your peaceful spirit stay in our homes so that we may feel good about each other, we pray... Father hear our prayer.

Father, help us to enjoy and appreciate the work we do in offices, homes and schools, we pray ... Father hear our prayer.

Father, help us to have the hope that we can make the world a better place, we pray... Father, hear our prayer.

SONG LEADER   Like the Brute Family, when we leave here today remember to keep the good feeling in our homes and carry it in our hearts all year long.

Let us conclude by singing "Joy, Joy, Joy" (*Hi God II*)

FISHING STORIES

(FIFTH SUNDAY OF THE YEAR—Winter)

Isaiah 6:1-2, 3-8   1 Corinthians 15:1-11   Luke 5:1-11

THEME
: We are all called to be "fishers of people" for the Lord

PROPS
: 1. Cardboard boat supported by wooden stands. (3 crates behind the boat. One oar or paddle. This will be used during the gospel.
  2. Fishing net filled with paper fish placed behind the boat and out of sight. Another empty net in front of the boat.
  3. Large paper picture of two or more fishermen in in a boat hung on the wall behind the boat.
  4. Large maps of Israel, India and New York City for use during the lesson. These can be placed on an easel.
  5. Small maps of your local community or area surrounding your church. These will be distributed to children after the lesson.
  6. Lesson costumes: A robe for "Peter," a white sheet or robe with a blue stripe for "Mother Teresa," a black shirt and clerical collar for "Fr. Ritter."

PERSONNEL
: 1. Presenter
  2. Song Leader
  3. Prayer Leader
  4. Reader
  5. Gospel Pantomime Actors: "Jesus," "Simon," "Andrew."
  6. A narrator and 2 students readers: "Jesus" and "Simon."
  7. Lesson Actors. "Peter," "Mother Teresa," and "Fr. Ritter" are part of the lesson presentation.

(If you have a large congregation, a separate microphone must be used for each reader.)

GREETING

PRESENTER
: Good morning. I would like to extend a warm welcome to our visitors. As we begin this celebration let us think about how we are all called to be disciples of our Lord. Today we will come to understand more deeply what that means.

OPENING PRAYER

PRAYER LEADER   We have all failed at times to respond to God. Let us now ask God's forgiveness.
Lord, forgive us for the times we have turned our eyes and hearts away from the poor and needy.
Forgive us for the times we did not appreciate the talents and gifts you have given us, and, for the times that we seek not your will but our own. Amen.

FIRST READING

READER   Isaiah 6:1-2, 3-8

SONG LEADER   "Here I Am" (*Glory and Praise*)

GOSPEL

PRESENTER   Today we will not only hear but also see the word of God. I invite the children to come up and sit on the floor.

(Jesus is facing the congregation as if teaching. The fishermen, using mime, are washing their nets in front of their boat.)

PRESENTER   A reading from the holy gospel according to Luke.

As the crowd pressed in on Jesus to hear the word of God, he saw two boats moored by the side of the lake; the fishermen had disembarked and were washing their nets.

(Jesus turns from the crowd and shades his eyes as he peers in the direction of the boats. The fishermen continue to wash their nets.)

PRESENTER   He got into one of the boats, the one belonging to Simon, and asked him to pull out a short distance from the shore;

(Jesus climbs into the boat and picks up their net, points toward the wall at the rear of the boat and then sits down. Simon and Andrew climb into the boat and row briefly.)

PRESENTER   Then, remaining seated, he continued to teach the crowds from the boat. When he had finished speaking, he said to Simon:

JESUS	"Put out into deep water and lower your nets for a catch."
SIMON	"Master, we have been hard at it all night long and have caught nothing; but if you say so, I will lower the nets."
PRESENTER	Upon doing this they caught such a great number of fish that their nets were at the breaking point. *(Peter and Andrew lower their nets and pull up a second net with fish attached to the net.)*
PRESENTER	They signaled to their mates in the other boat to come and help them. *(Peter and Andrew wave to the men in the other boat—picture on wall.)*
PRESENTER	They came, and together they filled the two boats until they nearly sank. At the sight of this, Simon Peter fell at the knees of Jesus . *(Simon kneels in "boat" with his head on Jesus' lap.)*
SIMON	"Leave me, Lord. I am a sinful man."
PRESENTER	For indeed, amazement at the catch they had made seized him and all his shipmates, as well as James and John, Zebedee's sons, who were partners with Simon.
JESUS	"Do not be afraid. From now on you will be catching people." *(Jesus lifts Simon's head and pats his back with a proud gesture.)*
PRESENTER	With that they brought their boats to land, left everything, and became his followers. *(The fishermen row a few strokes. Then Jesus gets out of the boat followed by the others and leaves the worship space.)*
PRESENTER	This is the gospel of the Lord!

LESSON

PRESENTER Did you hear what Jesus said to Peter in the boat? He said, "You will be catching people." What do you think that means, "catching people"? (*response*) We have Peter here. Let's ask him if we're right. Peter can you help us?

(Peter comes forward to the microphone, bringing a map of the area he worked in. He should place the map of Israel on an easel. The presenter sits down to listen.)

PETER "Yes, you're right, Jesus asked us twelve men to go out among all the peoples and gather them to him. No longer would I be catching fish in the Sea of Galilee. This was now my fishing territory. (*Points to Jerusalem.*) I began my work in Jerusalem in Palestine. It was sort of the headquarters for the new church. Later in my life I traveled to Rome to guide the church there.

How did I do my fishing? I preached to anyone who would listen about Jesus, about the great love he had for me and all people. I healed the sick and baptized those who then believed. It was harder work than catching fish, but the best work of my life!

(Mother Teresa enters walking to presenter and Peter saying:)

MOTHER TERESA That's how I feel. It's the most rewarding work of my life! Hello. Hello, Peter. (*addressing the congregation*) Most people know me as Mother Teresa. Jesus calls me too to be a "catcher of people." I didn't hear him with my ears, as you did, Peter, but I heard his call in my heart when I was a young girl. He called me to this country (*sets up map of India*), India. Can you say India? (*children repeat*) The city of Calcutta. (*points to city*) This is *my* fishing territory.

I became a sister teaching wealthy High School girls in Calcutta. But, children, when I saw the thousands of poor, sick people living, eating, and even dying right on the streets, I heard God's call to gather these people to him, to help them. Every day my fellow sisters and I go out in the streets and bring the dying back to one of our homes so they may die in dignity. We help the lepers earn a living and we save many babies that are abandoned. These people do not know me, but I see Jesus' face in every one of theirs. I am so happy God called me.

(Fr. Ritter enters saying:)

FR. RITTER   Did someone mention people on the streets? (*shakes hands*) Hello, Peter, and Mother Teresa. (*sets up map of New York City*) The streets of New York City are my fishing territory. I'm Fr. Bruce Ritter. The people I gather are runaway teenagers. Many, many unhappy kids leave their homes and come to New York City. (*bending down to the kids*) Did you ever feel like running away from home? We all want to run away at some time, but these kids actually did it.

They come to big cities like New York and walk the streets, hanging out, not having a place to stay. Many turn to drugs and alcohol for comfort. I run a house called the Covenant House. (*Can you all say Covenant House?*) We help about 1000 teens a month with counseling, and medical care, and try to get them home. My job is a hard one too, but I love it.

PRESENTER   Thank you to all three of you for sharing your fishing stories. Children all of us are called by God to gather people. Where do you think your "fishing territory" is? (*response*) Some day you may hear God call you in your heart to go to another place, perhaps another country to do God's work. But now our fishing territory begins right here in _____ (*name of your city and church*), in the schools you attend, and in your neighborhoods. By the way you talk and act and the good deeds you do, people will see God's love for them.

Today my helpers have a map for each of you. Please look it over with your families, find your home and school. When you pray tonight ask Jesus' help in being good "catchers of people."

You may all return to your seats now.

COMMUNAL PRAYER

PRAYER LEADER   Please respond: "Lord, hear our prayer."

That we may show our loving Father to others by our good example, we pray ... Lord, hear our prayer.
That our faith grows in strength, enabling us to be true "fishers of people" for the Lord, we pray ... Lord, hear our prayer.
Bless the work of Fr. Ritter's Covenant House and Mother Teresa's Sisters of Charity, we pray ... Lord, hear our prayer.

SONG LEADER   "Come Along With Me to Jesus" (*Hi God II*)

IN TOUCH WITH GOD

(THIRD SUNDAY OF LENT—Spring)
TRANSFIGURATION

Exodus 3:1-8, 13-15   1 Corinthians 10:1-6, 10-12   Luke 13: 1-9

THEME   Being with God through prayer

PROPS
1. Praying hands silhouette on a back wall or in a place where everyone can see.
2. The gospel is to be illustrated. We suggest 3 pictures: 1) Jesus praying with face and clothes glowing in glory. 2) Jesus standing with Moses on one side and Elijah the prophet on the other. 3) Jesus standing alone with a large cloud above him and several apostles are crouched in fear. You may use the "Help, I Can't Draw" books published by Augsburg to compose the pictures you desire; or look through Bible picture books and enlarge them or ask an artist to draw them. The pictures will be changed by an older child.
3. A marker and a large sheet of paper on an easel under the pictures.
4. Prayer cards in the shape of praying hands are to be given to the children after the celebration. Prayer example: Lord sometimes it's hard for me to pray because I can't see you. I want to be good, to be like you. Help me to hear you. Amen.

PERSONNEL
1. Presenter
2. Song Leader
3. Prayer Leader
4. Reader
5. Two children to help with the Opening Prayer

GREETING

PRESENTER   Welcome to you all. We come together to celebrate our shared belief in God, to pray together. Let us begin this celebration by asking ourselves, "How do we pray?"

OPENING MEDITATION

CHILD 1   I'm seven years old. I don't really understand much about God. I don't know what to say to God. When I'm older, I'll pray more because then I'll understand.

CHILD 2   I'm 10 years old and keeping very active with my homework, learning to swim, playing soccer, watching my favorite TV programs, using my computer. I know God loves me, but I don't think it's too important to sit down and pray.

CHILD 1   I'm seventeen and keep a very busy schedule with school, clubs, part-time job, dating. God in my life? Don't think about it much. Do I pray? Not really…mostly at meals with the family.

CHILD 2   I'm thirty-five, a busy homemaker, trying to juggle lots of things, driving the kids places, keeping the house tidy, cooking, working part time. To tell you the truth, I'm just too exhausted at the end of the day to pray.

CHILD 1   I'm seventy-two years old. I'm not so busy any more. Seems like you and me, God, have been strangers. Not in the habit of talking to you. Can't teach an old dog new tricks, you know.

PRESENTER   Heavenly Father, teach us to pray. Open our ears and hearts so that we know you are here. Amen.

FIRST READING

READER   Exodus 3:1-8, 13-15

SONG LEADER   "Wherever I Am God is" *(Hi God III)*

PRE-GOSPEL COMMENTS

PRESENTER   Will the children come up now so that you can see the gospel today as well as hear it. Please sit on the floor in front of me.

(As the gospel of the Transfiguration is read, three pictures representing the story will be shown.)

GOSPEL

PRESENTER   Luke 13:1-9

LESSON

PRESENTER   I have noticed that when two people are close friends and spend a lot of time with each other, sometimes they act like the other person. Have you ever noticed that? Sometimes it's just a way of laughing, or an expression they use. (*Example: One friend likes to say "super" when she likes something. Soon she is also saying "super" when she is pleased*.) This happens a lot with husbands and wives. Do you use any expressions that your moms and dads use? (*Wait for a response*.)

In today's gospel Jesus went up the mountain to pray. And we heard what happened, didn't we? The gospel writer said Jesus' face glowed and his robes were a dazzling white. The apostles even saw God's chosen men, Moses and Elijah, appear! Jesus was spending time with his Father. He was being very close to him. (*Refer back to picture 1*.) So close, in fact, I think Jesus became like his Father then. He was so close to God then in prayer that he actually showed the Father's Glory—just glowing with it. The more Jesus prayed and worked in His lifetime, the closer he came to God.

Do you pray? (*response*) When do you pray? (*response*) Do you like making up your own prayers, using your own words? (*response*) What memorized prayers do you know? (*response*) Do you know the meaning of all the words you used in the memorized prayer?

(*Perhaps you can recount the story about the little boy who thought the prayer was "Hail Mary, full of grapes!"*)

Let's make a prayer right now (*Remove the gospel pictures and expose the paper underneath. Pick up magic marker*.) You tell me what to write and we'll make a prayer for all of us to pray.

(*You may want to start them out with Dear God...after the prayer is composed, the whole congregation will recite it with you*.)

Did you know that you can pray without saying or thinking a word? Yes, you can just sit and be with God. And God can talk to you.

Try that some time. Lie on your bed or sit on the floor in your bedroom. Get quiet, close your eyes, and sit with God awhile. It may seem odd at first but keep at it and you will experience God's presence.

I don't know if our clothes will change color like the story about Jesus, but we will become more like God if we spend time with God. Why don't we try it this week?

COMMUNAL PRAYER

PRAYER LEADER   Please respond, "Lord, teach us to pray."

Help us to make time for you in our lives, we ask of the Lord... Lord, teach us to pray.

Help us to rely not so much on ourselves but on you, we ask of the Lord ... Lord, teach us to pray.

Create in us the desire to be like you, to love like you, to heal like You, we ask of the Lord ... Lord, teach us to pray.

CLOSING

SONG LEADER   Children, as you leave church today make sure you pick up a prayer card we have for you.

"Receive Our Prayer" (*Hi God III*)

STICKS AND STONES

(FIFTH SUNDAY OF LENT—Spring)

Isaiah 43:16-21   Philippians 3: 8-14   John 8: 1-11

THEME   Accepting others

PROPS   1. Sign on the wall or easel that says, "Sticks and Stones... "

2. Rocks approximately 3" to 4" across, with paper strips imprinted with derogatory words such as stupid, jerk, fatso, clumsy, etc. glued on them, are placed on the floor and used during the gospel enactment and lesson. You should have enough extra rocks so that each child will be able to take one home.

3. Excerpt from the book "Blubber" (Judy Blume) to be read during the lesson. You will use pages 8-9, beginning with "As Linda climbed... "

PERSONNEL   1. Presenter

2. Song Leader

3. Prayer Leader

4. 2 Readers

5. 9 children to pantomime the roles of Scribe, Pharisee, 3 crowd members, woman, Jesus and 2 students.

GREETING

PRESENTER   Welcome. God created you and God loves you; because of this you are special. Today in our celebration we ask God to help us to respect other people and to learn to accept them just the way they are.

OPENING PRAYER

PRESENTER   Father in heaven, the love of your Son led him to accept the suffering of the cross so that his brothers and sisters might have a life. Change our selfishness into self-giving. Help us to accept the world you have given us that we may change the darkness into the life and joy of Easter.

FIRST READING

READER   Isaiah 43:16-21

SONG LEADER   "Thank You, God for Being so Good" (*CTWWS*)

GOSPEL

PRESENTER   Today John's gospel will be heard and seen. I invite the children to come up and sit on the floor.

(This enactment would be more effective if the actors could speak their parts, but because of difficulty hearing in a large room, the actors will pantomime and call out non-Scripture lines, two readers plus thePresenter will read the Scripture at microphones. Two actors are dressed richly. The rest of the crowd are holding rocks.)

PRESENTER   Early in the morning, Jesus was in the Temple area teaching. A Scribe and a Pharisee, leading a group of angry people came up to Jesus. They had with them a woman who was caught sinning in adultery.

(Jesus and two other actors are sitting center stage. Jesus is miming teaching, gesturing with his hands. When the others approach, Jesus stands. The woman stands in the rear, hands tied, her head is down. The Pharisee is standing next to the Scribe who is holding a book in one hand. He beckons Jesus to come closer. First he points at the woman, then he jabs his finger at a page in the book acting very angry.)

READER I   Teacher, we have found this woman breaking a law of Moses. It says in the law that a woman breaking this law would be stoned to death as punishment. What do you say about the case?

CROWD ACTORS   *(calling out at random)* "That's right"! "Stone her! " "She deserves it." "It's the law!" "What do you say, Jesus?"

PRESENTER   They were posing this question to trap Jesus. Jesus simply bent down and began tracing his finger in the sand.

(Jesus bends over and doodles in front of him ... like drawing in the sand.)

CROWD ACTORS	*(calling out at random)* "What did he say?" "What's he doing?" "Come on, are we going to stone her?" "She's guilty!"
PRESENTER	When they persisted in their questioning, Jesus straightened up. *(Jesus picks up a rock and offers it to the crowd and the whole congregation.)*
READER II	Let the person among you who has committed no sin be the first one to throw a stone at her.
PRESENTER	Jesus bent down again and began drawing in the sand. The crowd drifted away one by one, beginning with the elders. Only the woman remained. She stood there before him. *(The crowd reacts: drop stones, hang their heads, and leave. Jesus gets up and walks over to the woman, untying her hands.)*
READER II	It seems they all have left. No one has condemned you, have they?
READER I	No one, sir.
READER II	Neither will I. *(holding both of her upper arms, looking into her face)*
READER II	You may go. But, from now on avoid this sin. *(Woman shakes her head yes, kneels down and kisses his hand, and then runs off.)*
PRESENTER	This is the gospel of the Lord.

LESSON

PRESENTER	Thanks to all of those actors and readers for helping to make the gospel come alive for us. I would like the rest of you to come up a bit closer. First pick up one of the rocks lying here. In today's gospel, a woman was caught breaking a law of Moses, right? What was the legal punishment for that law? *(See if anyone remembers.)* Yes, it was stoning. Two thousand years ago, many punishments were very cruel. A person

could be stoned to death for breaking certain laws.

Jesus knew the laws and knew the punishment due...but what did he say to the angry crowd? Did he say "Yes, you have the right to stone her. Go right ahead?" *(response)* No, he said "Let the person among you that has no sin throw the first stone." Why do you think he said that? *(response)* Yes, and that Jesus doesn't want us to condemn, to judge another person harshly.

We ask ourselves today, are we like the people in the crowd. I don't see too many physical rocks being thrown around, but I do think we throw a different type of rock. It's called a "put-down" or "name-calling." What put-downs are written on these rocks? *(Have the children read as many as possible.)* Do you hear these names in school or out playing? *(response)* Have you ever heard the saying "Sticks and stones will break my bones, but names will never hurt me"? Do you think that's always true?

I want to read an episode from a book about a girl named Linda. Linda is a fifth grader who is fat. She is riding home from school in the bus.

(Read excerpt from Blubber by Judy Blume, pages 8-9, beginning with "As Linda climbed... ")

Linda was hurt wasn't she? Name calling does hurt. We adults are name callers, too. In our daily driving, or shopping, or working with someone who doesn't think or act like us, we give out put-downs. Maybe the person doesn't hear us, but the stones are thrown, disturbing the peace within ourselves, injuring even the people who are in our company.

Each of us has our own bad points. We don't want them pointed out, to be judged.

During this lenten season, let us leave the rocks we received today on our bedroom dressers, as a help to examine our consciences. Let us ask ourselves every evening. "Have I been accepting of my classmates, my brothers and sisters, my co-workers, or do I throw stones? "

COMMUNAL PRAYER

PRAYER LEADER   Please respond, "Lord, hear our prayer."

Lord, help us to value our friends and neighbors, we pray to the Lord ... Lord, hear our prayer.

Lord, help us to find the words to make others feel good, we pray to the Lord ... Lord hear our prayer.

Lord, we pray for all our brothers and sisters that we don't know, those who are sick, those who don't have homes, the hungry and the poor, we pray to the Lord...Lord, hear our prayer.

SONG LEADER   "A Wondrous Work of Art" (*Hi God III*)

EASTER RAINBOWS

(EASTER—Spring)

Acts 10:34, 37-43   John 20:1-9

THEME | The sign of a rainbow. The promise is fulfilled: we have everlasting life.

PROPS
1. A cardboard tomb with a white cloth inside. A rainbow above it or on the wall nearby.
2. Rainbow shakers to be used by the children during the lesson. These shakers can be made by using multi-colored tissue paper fringed and attached to a small dowel. Roll these up in white tissue paper and place them in a basket in the sanctuary.
3. A basket for "Mary" used during the gospel narrative.
4. An "Alleluia" banner to be placed in a stand or hung up in the sanctuary.

PERSONNEL
1. Presenter
2. Song Leader
3. Prayer Leader
4. Reader
5. 3 speakers
6. Adult helpers to pass out shakers.

GREETING

PRESENTER | Easter greetings to all of you! Today is a rainbow celebration! A rainbow is a symbol of hope. Jesus is our hope. He is the promise come true. His Spirit fills us with his new life! Let us close our eyes for a moment and thank God for giving us his Son.

OPENING PRAYER

PRAYER LEADER | Heavenly Father, how happy we are today! You made a promise to send your Son, your love, in human form, to free us from sin. You have kept that promise. You have raised him from the dead. We will praise and thank you forever and ever for loving us so. Amen.

FIRST READING

READER	Acts 10:34, 37-43 *(Use the actor Peter in the gospel to proclaim this reading.)*
PRESENTER	"New Hope" *(Hi God II)*

GOSPEL NARRATIVE

(The Presenter is the narrator of the gospel. The actors interject the characters' feelings between the lines. The children are called up front to see better.)

PRESENTER	Early in the morning, on the first day of the week, while it was still dark outside, Mary Magdalene walked to the cemetery to visit Jesus's tomb.

(Mary walks toward the tomb, carrying a basket.)

MARY	I can't sleep well lately. Jesus is dead. My heart is so troubled. If I just sit near his tomb awhile, perhaps I'll feel more peace.

(Mary sits down near the tomb for a moment and then walks in front of the tomb.)

PRESENTER	When she reached the tomb, she was surprised to see that the stone door was moved.
MARY	Oh my goodness! Why is the stone moved? Have they stolen his body? I've got to tell Peter!

(Mary drops her basket, looks surprised, and then she runs off.)

PRESENTER	So off she ran to tell the news to Peter and John.

(Mary calls out Peter and John's names while she running.)

MARY	The Lord has been taken from the tomb and I don't know where they have put him.
PETER	It's not even daybreak yet! Who would have moved the stone? What does this mean?

JOHN	Well let's not stand here guessing. Let's go!
PRESENTER	Peter and John ran to the cemetery. John got there first but didn't go in. Peter, the leader of the apostles, went in. (*pause until actor has cloth in his hands.*) He found the wrapping that covered Jesus' head lying on the floor. (*Peter exits the tomb, holding the cloth for all to see.*)
PETER	He's not here! These are the wrappings that Jesus was buried in. It is as he said. He's alive!!
PRESENTER	Then the other disciple went in. He saw and believed.
PETER AND JOHN	He is alive. Let's spread the news! (*All 3 actors run off.*)
PRESENTER	This is the gospel of the Lord.

LESSON

PRESENTER	Before we talk about the the Easter gospel, my helpers have something to give you. (*Adult helpers pass out the rolled-up shakers.*) You can open them now. Do you know what they are? Shakers. Right! Do you know what they're usually used for? (*responses: football games, cheerleading, parades*) They're used to show spirit and excitement. They're good for a day like today. Today is the most special day of the year! What are we excited about today? (*responses: It's Easter, Jesus lives, We got candy in our baskets, new clothes*) Yes, Jesus is alive and he will never leave us! Let's show that we are excited today by using our shakers. (*Waits for some waving.*) That's good! Now hold your shakers still for a moment. Let's look at our banner. It says "Alleluia." Did you know that "Alleluia" is an exciting word? It means "Praise to God." Let's say that together, "Praise to God!" Good! Now whenever I say the word "Alleluia," you help me to praise God by waving your shakers. Okay? Ready? I noticed that everything in springtime shouts "Alleluia" to God! When Jesus died and rose from the dead, he gave us a new life, and because of that new life we pray "Alleluia." All of nature shares in this new "Alleluia" life. What do you see

in spring that shows signs of "new life"? (Budding trees, flowers blooming, eggs hatching, and baby bunnies.) If the spirits of these creatures could speak, I'm sure they would shout "Alleluia" too! How good it is to feel this Easter excitement! Let us remember to praise God all day and every day with our "Alleluias"!

COMMUNAL PRAYER

PRAYER LEADER   Our response will be "Jesus our hope, hear us! "
That the feelings of joy and togetherness we have at this Celebration be shared with our families and friends throughout the day, we pray to the Lord...Jesus our hope, hear us.
That our brothers and sisters of all the nations in the world experience peace, we pray to the Lord...Jesus our hope, hear us.
That the families troubled by illness, whether emotional or physical be comforted in Easter hope, we pray to the Lord...Jesus our hope, hear us.

CLOSING

SONG LEADER   "Color the World" (*CTWWS*)

A NEW CREATION

(EASTER—Spring)

Acts 10: 34, 37-43   John 20: 1-9

THEME
We will live again! Through Jesus' resurrection we become a new creation

PROPS
1. Plastic "Alleluia" eggs with yarn strings are hidden under the chairs or pews. As the children find the eggs, invite them to hang them on the trees behind a cardboard "tomb." The trees are branches inserted in plaster-filled buckets.

2. The gospel is narrated by the presenter and pantomimed by three student actors in the style of a "cantata." The actors' feelings will be interjected with the actor chanting his or her lines and the congregation repeating the chant.

3. The story "The Caterpillar's Journey" is narrated during the lesson. 8 pictures of the story can be made into a huge book (3'x3') which is held by an easel. Two students will turn the pages of the book and add the pictures of the wind when necessary. A furry stuffed caterpillar and a cocoon made from white netting and a tissue butterfly are used by the presenter.

4. The children are given ribbon butterflies with pins attached to the back. They are wrapped in tissue as if in cocoons.

PERSONNEL
1. Presenter
2. Song Leader
3. Prayer Leader
4. 3 children to take the parts of Mary Magdalene, Peter, and John. Mary and Peter sing their lines. Peter will do the first reading.
5. 2 students to turn pages of book.

GREETING

PRESENTER
Easter blessings to all of you. Today is the greatest holiday of the year. There are signs of Easter life all around us: the beautiful flowers, the Alleluia eggs you put on our trees. But, most of all (*gesturing*), all of you are the greatest sign of Jesus' life! Let us bow our heads for a moment, close our eyes, and thank Jesus for his saving grace.

OPENING PRAYER

PRESENTER   Heavenly Father, what great joy we have today! Jesus is alive. He is with us and will never leave us. We thank you and praise you, Father, for your Son and our new life, forever and ever. Amen.

FIRST READING

(Today the reader will take on the role of Peter.)

READER   As you know, I, Peter, one of the twelve apostles, traveled with and learned from Jesus for three years until his death and resurrection. I repeat for you the same testimony that I proudly proclaimed, as written in the Acts of the Apostles.

Acts 10:34, 37-43

SONG LEADER   "Signs of New Life," verses 1 and 3

GOSPEL NARRATIVE

(The children are called forward before the reading of the Gospel.)

PRESENTER   Early in the morning on the first day of the week, while it was still dark, Mary Magdalene was walking to the tomb.

(Mary's song is to the tune of "Peace Is Flowing," Hi God I)

MARY   We're so lost, so lost without him,
We don't know what to do
We're so lost, so lost without him
Feeling all alone and blue.

ALL   *(Sing these lines.)*

PRESENTER   When she came to Jesus' tomb she saw that the stone door has been moved away. So Mary ran off to Simon Peter and the other disciple and told them: "The Lord has been taken from the tomb and we don't know where they have put him."

(After running to where Peter and John are standing, Mary

sings the following to the tune of "Are Not Our Hearts,"Hi God I.)

MARY   Peter and John, please do hurry! Peter and John, please come quick! My head's in a whirl. My heart's in a flurry! Peter and John, please come quick!

ALL   *(Sing the same lines)*

PRESENTER   Peter and the other disciple ran to the tomb. They ran side by side. The disciple reached the tomb first. He did not enter but bent down to peer in. He saw the wrappings lying on the ground. Soon Simon Peter came along.

(Peter looks at the opened entrance in disbelief and sings the following to the tune of "Come Along With Me," Hi GOD II.)

PETER   I don't really understand it.
What can this mean?
I don't really understand it.
Can it be just what it seems?

ALL   *(Sing these lines.)*

PRESENTER   Peter then entered the tomb. He saw the wrappings on the ground and saw the piece of cloth that had covered Jesus' head, not lying with the wrappings, but rolled up in a place by itself.

(Peter sings the following to the tune of "Oh Yes, Lord Jesus Lives," Hi God II.)

PETER   I do believe that he is risen! Alle, Alle, Alleluia! The Lord is risen. The Lord is risen. Alle, Alle, Alleluia!

ALL   *(Sing these lines.)*

PRESENTER   Then the disciple who had arrived first at the tomb went in. He saw and believed.

(The following is sung by John, Peter, and Mary to the tune of "Oh Yes, Lord Jesus Lives," Hi God II.)

JOHN, PETER & MARY	The Lord is risen. The Lord is risen. Alle, Alle, Alleluia. The Lord is risen. The Lord is risen. Alle, Alle, Alleluia.
ALL	*(Sings these lines.)*
PRESENTER	This is the gospel of the Lord!

LESSON

PRESENTER	St. Peter just proclaimed, "Jesus is alive! He is risen!" This is good news for followers of Jesus. Are there any followers of Jesus here? Raise your hands. *(response)* This is good news for us! I am going to tell you a story called, "The Caterpillar's Journey" that will help explain why Jesus' resurrection is such good news.

(Narrates "The Caterpillar's Journey" with students turning the pages of the oversized book on the easel. The students add a picture of the wind to the painting twice during the story.)

THE CATERPILLAR'S JOURNEY

(The first page of the book is a picture of a caterpillar looking at daisy.)

Once upon a time a lazy brown caterpillar started out on a journey. You would not have thought it a long journey—just across the road and under the fence to the roots of the big maple tree. But the caterpillar thought it a long way and full of dangers.

He saw a tall white daisy on the other side of the road, and he thought he would stop and talk to her. It took him a long, long time to cross the road.

(Please turn the page. The picture is of a caterpillar and a robin by a dead stalk.)

When at last he came to the place where he had seen the daisy, he found only a tall brown stalk. "Where is she?" he asked a robin that was nearby looking for worms. "She is dead—she is dead" answered the robin in a little song. "Oh," said the caterpillar, "I want to talk to her."

(Please turn the page. The picture is of a leafless tree and brown grass.)

The wind was singing in a soft gentle voice, "She will live again—she will live again." "Well, where is the friendly green grass? Oh, I shall miss it so." The robin sang, "It is dead."

"Oh, my, the big maple tree is dead too," sighed the caterpillar with regret.

(Wind is added.)

But again he heard the soft whisper of the wind, "They shall live again—they shall live again."

(Please turn the page. Picture of cocoon making.)

But the caterpillar did not understand, and he felt very sad as he began his cocoon. "They are dead," he kept saying to himself. Soon the cocoon was finished, and the caterpillar, ready for his long nap, was all snug and warm in his winter house.

(Please turn the page. Picture of 2 children looking at the cocoon.)

He did not hear the two children who came and looked at the cocoon and said to each other, "The caterpillar is dead."

(Wind is added.)

But the wind heard them and whistled, "He shall live again—he shall live again. Wait and see."

The cold wind and snow came and stayed all winter. The wind no longer whispered in a soft voice but whistled shrilly through the trees.

(Please turn the page. Picture is of a spring scene.)

By and by the sun grew warm and bright, the snow melted, and the early crocuses appeared, growing through the snow. Little seeds began to grow in the warm earth and soon there were violets, daisies, and even some Jack-in-the-pulpits. All was lovely and green again.

Something began to happen to the cocoon in which the caterpillar went to sleep. Slowly it opened, and something moved inside.

(Wind is added.)

The wind saw it and said softly, "The caterpillar is alive again." Then out of the cocoon came a funny wet thing, not at all like the brown caterpillar.

(Please turn the page. Picture of a butterfly on a branch.)

The sun shone warmly upon it, and soon it was resting there on the big maple tree, a large beautiful butterfly with wings of brown and gold.

The butterfly did not understand. "I thought I was a caterpillar."

(Turn the page. A picture of the butterfly with the daisy, a tree and a robin.)

Then, the caterpillar/butterfly thought of his friends, the lovely white daisy, the friendly green grass, the robin, and the big maple tree. He looked around him and there they were, everyone very beautiful, in the warm sunlight.

He did not understand, nobody understands, but we know it's true. "They shall live again—they shall live again."

PRESENTER   What did the wind whisper about the daisy, about the tree, and about the caterpillar? *(response)* Yes. "They will live again—they will live again." God's Spirit is like the wind in our story. His message on this Easter morning is the same. You will live again—you will live again!

We can imagine ourselves as caterpillars on this earth *(picks up furry caterpillar)*: warm, wooly creatures creeping and munching our way through life. And like our friend in the story, we can be troubled and even afraid of the problems in our world. We are sad when our grandparents or other relatives and friends die. We may think of death as an end, like this cocoon is the end of the caterpillar's life.

(Place the caterpillar into the cocoon and leave it in a prominent place.)

But Jesus promises new life! On Easter Sunday, Jesus was raised from his tomb. (*motioning toward cardboard tomb*) His father raised him to a new and glorified life. The good news is that we share in this glorified life. Our death will not be an end, but a change. Like a caterpillar changing to a beautiful and free butterfly (*lifts up the butterfly*).

Let us thank Jesus for giving us this new life by singing our message as we did in the gospel. _____ will sing the line and then we will repeat it.

SONG LEADER   (*Sings refrain from "Thank You God" (Hi God I) and the children repeat it.*)

We have little cocoons with a sign of Jesus' new life inside. Please open these with your parents and have them pin the butterfly on you so that we may enjoy their beauty too.

(*The organist or other musicians may play the above melody as background music while the cocoons are being handed out.*)

COMMUNAL PRAYER

PRAYER LEADER   Our response today is "Living Jesus, hear us."

Fill us with your joy so that we may pass on this gift to everyone we meet today, we pray to you...Living Jesus, hear us.
Strengthen our families with hope, compassion and peace, we pray to you...Living Jesus, hear us.
Through your healing life in us, help us to comfort the sick,lonely parishioners, relatives, and neighbors of our community, we pray to you... Living Jesus, hear us.
We pray for our brothers and sisters everywhere, especially for those in countries where there is conflict, we pray to you... Living Jesus, hear us.

SONG LEADER   "This Is the Day" (*Hi God II*)

Permission has been granted by CBP Press, P. 0. Box 179, St. Louis, MO 63166 to reprint the words from the filmstrip, "The Caterpillar's Journey."

WORKING FOR THE LORD

(THIRD SUNDAY OF EASTER—Spring)

Acts 5:27-32,40-41   Revelation 5:11-14   John.21:1-19

THEME	Fed by the Lord, we can do his work.
PROPS	1. Several frames of a projected filmstrip depicting this gospel can be used while the gospel is being read. Or, pictures found in Bible story books can be enlarged. Use an opaque projector for this.
	2. Cardboard boat (8' long and 2' high)
	3. A net full of paper fish. Fish are made with 2 pieces of green or brown construction paper stapled together at the edges, leaving an opening. They are stuffed with tissue and then stapled closed. Label each fish with a Christian job: "Feed the hungry," "Comfort the sick and lonely," "Lead children to the Lord," "Spread the Good News to all." These will be used as handouts for the children after the lesson.
	4. Fake log fire with paper stuffed fish and loaf of bread placed near the lectern.
PERSONNEL	1. Presenter takes the role of narrator at gospel.
	2. Song Leader
	3. Prayer Leader
	4. Reader
	5. 3 readers taking the roles of Jesus and other disciples
	6. Man or older boy and woman or older girl to help during the lesson

GREETING

PRESENTER   Welcome to you, my brothers and sisters in Christ. Jesus supports us in all his work. He himself gives us the nourishment we need. Let us close our eyes and thank God for taking care of us.

OPENING PRAYER

PRESENTER   Heavenly Father, you shared your life with us through your son, Jesus, who is always with us. Through him we do our life's work and we thank and praise you, Father, forever and ever. Amen.

READING

SONG LEADER "Wherever I Am, God Is" *(Hi God III)*

GOSPEL

(The children are invited to come up to the front and be seated before the gospel is proclaimed.)

PRESENTER A reading from the holy gospel according to John (21:1-19). At the sea of Tiberias Jesus showed himself to the disciples once again. This is how the appearance took place. Assembled were Simon Peter, Thomas, Nathaniel, Zebedee's sons, and two other disciples.

PETER "I am going out to fish."

DISCIPLES "We will join you, Peter."
(Project or show picture of men by the boat talking.)

PRESENTER They went off to get into their boat. All through the night they caught nothing. Just after daybreak Jesus was standing on the shore, though none of the disciples knew it was Jesus. Jesus called out to them.

(Project or show picture of Jesus on shore; men in boats.)

JESUS "Children, have you caught anything to eat?"

DISCIPLES "Not a thing!"

JESUS "Cast your net off to the starboard side, and you will find something."

PRESENTER So they made a cast, and took so many fish they could not haul the net in. Then the disciple Jesus loved cried out to Peter.

DISCIPLE "It is the Lord!"

PRESENTER	On hearing it was the Lord, Simon Peter threw on some clothes, and jumped into the water.
	(Project or show picture of Peter swimming ashore.)
	Meanwhile the other disciples came in the boat, towing the net full of fish. Actually, they were not far from land—no more than a hundred yards.
	When they landed, they saw a charcoal fire there with a fish laid on it and some bread. Jesus told them...
JESUS	"Bring some of the fish you just caught."
PRESENTER	Simon Peter went aboard and hauled ashore the net loaded with sizeable fish, one hundred fifty-three of them! In spite of the great number, the net was not torn. Jesus invited them.
JESUS	"Come and eat your meal."
	(Project or show picture of people eating the fish.)
PRESENTER	Not one of the disciples presumed to inquire, "Who are you?" for they knew it was the Lord. Jesus came over, took the bread and gave it to them, and did the same with the fish. This marked the third time that Jesus appeared to the disciples after being raised from the dead.
	This is the gospel of the Lord.

LESSON

PRESENTER	St. Peter and his friends caught a lot of fish in their net, didn't they? Do you think fish were important to them? *(response)* Yes! Fishing was their living, their work , their occupation. The people in their community could eat because of their fishing. In our gospel the apostles trusted in Jesus when he said they should cast their nets again and the outcome was fantastic! I think St. John, the writer of this gospel, has a message for us here at _____. It has to do with our jobs as Christians. *(walking back to the net of fish)* What type of fish are we to gather? What work are we to do in our community? Let's take a look at some of these fish. Maybe they'll give us a clue. *(taking one out of the net)* This one says....

(Fish have printed on them "Feed the hungry," "Clothe the naked," "Comfort the sick and lonely," "Lead children to the Lord," "Spread the Good News to all," "Help all to worship God with joyful Hearts," "Bring justice to all peoples." Have some of the older kids read some of the labels, with you repeating. Do others yourself.)

There are a lot of fish here—a lot of work for us. As in our gospel story, Jesus wants us to pull them in to accomplish this work. Who can do this?

(This should be rehearsed. At this time a man or an older boy comes up and tugs at the net, pretending that the net is very heavy. He shakes his head in defeat. Presenter then calls up a woman or an older girl. She tugs behind the man/boy with the same results. Finally, the Presenter calls up 3 or 4 children. The fish are finally pulled up!)

PRESENTER It looks like we all have to work together in our parish. A few can't do it alone. But do you know that all of us together *(gesturing to all present)* cannot accomplish this on our own effort. As in our gospel story, we must trust and be fed by the Lord. Jesus called the disciples to come ashore and eat fish and break bread *(lifting bread from the display)*. When they ate with Jesus, they truly recognized him, just as we see him in the eucharist. Every Sunday we come here to support each other and to share in the eucharist, our nourishment. This bread and wine gives us strength to do God's work. We come here again and again to be refueled, to share in Jesus' life. Only then can we do his work. So, before you go back to your seats, take one of the fish and sometime today ask your parents how you can best do the good work written on your fish.

COMMUNAL PRAYER

PRAYER LEADER Please respond, "Lord, hear our prayer."

Lord, help us to be sensitive to those in need in our parish, our community, and our world, we pray...Lord, hear our prayer.
Lord, help us to be generous with our time and talents so that we can do the work for which you have called us, we pray...Lord, hear our prayer.

Lord, you feed us. Help up feed those who are hungry in our world, we pray...Lord, hear our prayer.

CLOSING

SONG LEADER   "Living and Loving and Learning" *(Hi God III)*

UNITED AS ONE

(SEVENTH SUNDAY OF EASTER—Spring)

Acts 7:55-60   Revelation 22:12-14, 16-17, 20   John 17:20-26

THEME   Joining together, united in Christ

PROPS   1. A sign that says "Acts of the Apostles." This is used at the first reading.

2. The story of Swimmy by Leo Leonni (available at school or community libraries) will be used during the lesson with the help of a flannel board.

3. Flannel or tape-backed posterboard pictures of black Swimmy, 6-7 small red fish between clear contact paper, 6 separate red fish, 1 tuna, medusa, lobster, 3 angel fish, seaweed with rocks, eel, sea anemones, large rock formation with holes for little fish to hide. The tail portion of 2 large tunas for the final scene.

4. A large paper or cloth (3' x 5') imprinted with the quote from the gospel: "Father, may my followers be one... I living in them, you living in me...that their unity may be complete" is attached to the front of the altar cloth or taped on a wall during the lesson.

5. A fish cracker card with the same gospel quote on the back is given to the children as a handout. Cut out a fish pattern from posterboard and glue Pepperidge Farm fish on the front of it. Use a Pepperidge Farm pretzel fish as the eye. (This cracker fish will represent Swimmy). Advise the children not to eat the fish.

6. Sign saying "Avoid Evil" and another that says "Live Fully."

PERSONNEL   1. Presenter

2. Song Leader

3. Prayer Leader

4. Reader

5. 2 children to help put pictures on flannelboard

GREETING

PRESENTER   Welcome to all our parish family and guests. Let us be aware that we are one family together with Jesus as we share in this celebration.

OPENING PRAYER

PRAYER LEADER   Lord Jesus, you call us to support and care for each other, but often our selfishness keeps us apart. You sent your Holy Spirit to fill our hearts, and we are often not aware of this presence. Through your life and death you have taught us the way to live, but too often we choose the wrong path. Heal us and make us more like your son, Jesus. Amen.

FIRST READING

(Tape the sign on the front of the pulpit.)

READER   Our first reading is from a book of the New Testament called the Acts of the Apostles (7:55-60).

This book tells of the growth and trials of the early church community. Today we hear about St. Stephen being killed for his beliefs.

SONG LEADER   "Remember Your Love and Your Care" (CTWWS)

GOSPEL

PRESENTER   John 17:20-26

LESSON

PRESENTER   I invite the children to come up and sit on the floor by me. In this gospel of St. John, we heard Jesus at the Last Supper talking to his Father in heaven. He said many important things but the words that stand out the most to me are:

(At this time unroll, or gesture to, the large quote. Attach it to the front of the altar or tape on a wall.)

Father, may my followers be one...I living in them and you living in me...that their unity may be complete.

PRESENTER Let's all of us here read this together. (*The congregation reads the sign, too.*)

You can tell it's very important to Jesus that we, his followers, join together and be united.

I know a story called "Swimmy" that will help show why Jesus wants us to be united.

(The presenter narrates the story "Swimmy" by Leo Leonni, using the flannel board. Two children add and remove the pictures while he reads. This presentation must be practiced at least twice with the 2 children who are displaying the pictures so that the story is told smoothly.)

As the story is read, the appearance of pictures is as follows:

1. *Several red fish, adhered to clear contact paper, and Swimmy are on the board.*
2. *Tuna swoops down and is adhered on top of red.*
3. *Tuna and red fish are removed in one move.*
4. *Swimmy is placed near the center of the board.*
5. *Medusa is placed on board.*
6. *Lobster is added.*
7. *String of fish added.*
8. *Seaweed and rocks added.*
9. *Eel added.*
10. *Sea anemones added.*
11. *Remove several of the creatures. Add the rocks with hiding fish.*
12. *Put up configuration of partial fish without eye. Fish are on clear contact paper.*
13. *Add the rest of the fish by adding the individual red fish.*
14. *Add Swimmy as the eye.*
15. *Add tail portions of tunas.*

PRESENTER This could be a story about Jesus and us, couldn't it? Who do you think we are in this story? *(the red fish)* Who is Jesus? *(Swimmy)*

Swimmy became the group's eye. How is Jesus like our eye? Any suggestions? *(response)* He guides us through our lives.

Shows us the right way to go. Through him we can avoid evil *(put up sign)*, like the big tuna, and live fully *(putting up the sign)* without fear. With Jesus as our eye we can enjoy the world God gives us.

This is what Jesus wants for us, to stay together as one family, helping each other. We are happiest when we are united. We have a reminder of this lesson for you.

(Display the fish card with Pepperidge Farm fishes adhered to it; prayer is typed on the back.)

On the back is the same prayer we said in the beginning. Let's all of us pray it again.

(The whole congregation reads the prayer again. The children are sent back to their seats.)

COMMUNAL PRAYER

PRAYER LEADER   Please respond, "Lord, unite us."

Lord, help us to see the common bond in our family members and school friends so we may feel as one body, we pray ... Lord, unite us.

Lord, help us to see the world through Jesus' eyes: to find good and avoid evil, we pray... Lord, unite us.

Lord, help us be willing servants to all we meet, we pray... Lord, unite us.

CLOSING

SONG LEADER   "God Has Made Us a Family" *(Hi God III)*

THE LOST AND FOUND

(TWENTY-FOURTH SUNDAY OF THE YEAR—Fall)

Exodus 32:7-11, 13-14   1 Timothy 1:12-17   Luke 15:1-32

THEME
When you're lost, never give up! God is delighted every time we return to him.

PROPS
1. On a back wall or an easel are the words. "Lost and Found"
2. ID tags stating "I_____am a child of God. If I am lost, please return me to my Father." These are filled in with the children's names as they enter for the celebration.
3. Broom, apron, and coin for woman
4. Staff, tunic, head covering and a lamb (stuffed animal) for shepherd
5. A short examination of conscience card in the shape of a lamb will be given to the children after the lesson. Example: 1) Have I thought about God and talked to God today? 2) Have I helped anyone at school or home? 3) Did I yell at anyone or call them names? 4) Have I obeyed my parents and teachers cheerfully?
6. The children will need a song sheet with the song "Make a Joyful Noise" (CTWWS) for use during the gospel and the lesson.

PERSONNEL
1. Presenter
2. Song Leader
3. Prayer Leader
4. Reader
5. Woman and Shepherd

GREETING

PRESENTER
Welcome. Today we celebrate the joy God has when lost children return to God. Let us begin by reflecting on how good and safe we feel when we are walking with God.

OPENING PRAYER

PRAYER LEADER
Heavenly Father, how happy we are to gather here together as

one family. All of us, young and not so young, married, widowed, and single, need your love and forgiveness as our daily food. We thank and praise you, Father, for this never-ending gift through Jesus your son, forever and ever. Amen.

FIRST READING

READER   In our first reading we hear of a conversation between God and Moses. God is very upset with the Israelites. When Moses was away, they turned away from Him and were worshipping a pagan god. A reading from the book of Exodus (32:7-11, 13-14).

SONG LEADER   Leads everyone in "We Ask Your Forgiveness" (*Hi God III*).

GOSPEL

PRESENTER   All of us are going to help proclaim our gospel. Children, you may come up here by me now. Be sure to bring your song sheet.

The tax collectors and sinners were all gathering around to hear Jesus, at which the Pharisees and Scribes murmured, "This man welcomes sinners and eats with them." Then he told them this parable:

Suppose you were a shepherd and had a hundred sheep and lost one of them. What would you do? Doesn't a shepherd leave the ninety-nine in the open country and go after the lost sheep until he finds it?

(The shepherd enters looking around: near a plant, behind a chair etc, peering out at the congregation. He is wearing a rough-looking tunic and a head covering, and carries a staff. He walks to a microphone:)

SHEPHERD   I know it shouldn't bother me so, but I can't forget about this lost sheep. It's probably huddling under a rock someplace, too frightened to move. (Walks off into the congregation.)

Don't worry, little sheep! I won't give up until I find you. I'm a good shepherd. I'll get to you.

(Find the sheep under a predesignated chair/pew. This may have to be concealed so that the children won't see it when they enter.)

SHEPHERD	There you are! (*picking up the lamb and petting it gently*) It's all right. It's all right—you're home.
PRESENTER	That shepherd would put the sheep on his shoulders in jubilation and when he arrived home he'd invite his friends and neighbors to share in his joy.
	(*Shepherd goes back to the microphone. Gesturing with one arm and still holding the sheep he says:*)
SHEPHERD	Rejoice with me! I have found my lost sheep! Let us celebrate!
SONG LEADER	Leads in refrain of "Make a Joyful Noise" (*CTWWS*). (*Use clapping.*)
	(*The children will use their song sheets. The shepherds sits on the floor with the rest of the children.*)
PRESENTER	Suppose a woman had ten silver coins. If she lost one, wouldn't she light a lamp and sweep the house diligently until she finds it?
	(*During this narration a child playing the part of the woman enters with a broom and sweeps everywhere, even by the presenters feet, then she goes to the microphone.*)
WOMAN	I know I have nine more coins safe and sound but that 10th coin is missing and it just has to be here somewhere!
	(*This time she gets down on her hands and knees looking under the furniture. She finds it and then jumps up holding it up for everyone to see.*)
WOMAN	I knew I'd find it! I just knew it!
PRESENTER	She also calls to her neighbors and friends!
WOMAN	Hey, Joe! Hey, Mary! Rejoice with me! I've found my lost coin! Let's celebrate!
SONG LEADER	Leads in the refrain of "Make a Joyful Noise" (*CTWWS*) (*Use clapping.*)

PRESENTER Jesus then said: "I tell you, there will be the same kind of joy before the angels of God over one sinner who repents." This is the gospel of the Lord.

LESSON

PRESENTER Two things were lost in our gospel story. Who remembers what they were? (*response*) Have you ever lost or misplaced something in your home? Something like a special toy, or a favorite pair of earrings, or a library book that's overdue? You just know it has to be there. So you look and look and ask everybody and even clean up your shelves and drawers. You may even go back to the same spot two or three times! Then you may say, "I've spent enough time looking, I give up!" But you don't truly give up. It bothers you. Your eye is always on the lookout.

Then one day, there it is! It was hidden under the baseball cap, or caught in the rug behind the dresser. What joy, what smiles. No more worry, because you've found it! That is the feeling that Jesus speaks about today when one of God's children is lost and then found.

Who are God's children? (*response. Comment on the ID tags that the children are wearing. Ask the general congregation if any of God's children are out there. Ask for a show of hands*). Right! We're God's children, large and small. And, sometimes these children (*pointing to self*) get lost. We're like that sheep of the good shepherd. We're usually strolling and munching our way through life. We stay with the flock and follow the commands of the shepherd. We trust him. He's good for us. But sometimes we get careless, or stubborn, or selfish. We want to go on our own. So we turn away from the shepherd, from his way, and then we're lost.

When we break God's laws by being disobedient or unkind, when we tell lies, or take something that doesn't belong to us, we turn away from God, we sin.

Sometimes we may think, "See, I'm not very good. I don't feel like praying. I don't like helping out. I feel mean lots of the time. It's just too hard being like Jesus." But don't give up! Did the little sheep find its own way back to the shepherd, back to the flock? No! The shepherd came for it. The shepherd found it.

All we have to do is to want to follow Jesus, to say we're sorry and his Spirit does the rest and brings us home. Let's say "I'm sorry" in sign language.

(The sign for "I'm Sorry": Point to yourself with index finger and then make a circular motion with your fist on your chest.)

Then what rejoicing in heaven! Let us sing that rejoicing song that we sang in the gospel.

SONG LEADER   "Make a Joyful Noise" (*CTWWS*) (*Use clapping hands.*)

We have a little "daily review" that you can think over when you're saying your night prayers. Perhaps you can glue them on the back of your ID tag and keep them on your dresser.

COMMUNAL PRAYER

Our response today is, "We turn to you, Father."

That we may act like shepherds to our friends and family who are feeling sad or worried and bring them Jesus' joy we pray ...
We turn to you, Father.

That we may look for ways to help the poor and be concerned about the problems in other countries, we pray to the Lord...
We turn to you, Father

That we may examine ourselves to see in which way we are truly following you, we pray to the Lord... We turn to you, Father.

For those in our parish family that are sick. May they experience your healing power, we pray to the Lord ... We turn to you, Father.

SERVING ONE MASTER

(TWENTY-FIFTH SUNDAY OF THE YEAR—Fall)

Amos 8:4-7   1 Timothy 2:1-8   Luke 16:10-13

THEME Serving God, not wealth and fame

PROPS 1. Sign that says " Book of the Prophet Amos." This will be used at the first reading.

2. Transparencies or drawn enlargements (use an opaque projector) of "Jonathan's Gifts" by Bernice Stadler. See descriptions in lesson.

3. Heavy paper flutes with an imprinted prayer to be handed out at the end of the lesson. Each flute may have the name of a teacher on it if the teachers are being honored.

4. 4' cardboard figures of Mr. Money (a dollar bill with head, feet, and hands) and Mr. Important (boy with "I'm #1" on his T-shirt) for use during the lesson.

PERSONNEL 1. Presenter

2. Prayer Leader

3. Song Leader

4. Reader

5. Flutist

GREETING

PRESENTER Welcome. It is good to be gathered in God's name. In today's gospel we hear of two masters, God and money. As we begin today's celebration, let us pause right now and ask ourselves, "Whom do I serve?"

OPENING PRAYER

PRAYER LEADER Heavenly Father, you are the source of everything good. All that we are, all that we own is a gift from you. Let these gifts give you praise and glory through your son, Jesus. Amen.

FIRST READING

READER The First Reading is the Book of the Prophet Amos (8:4-7).

This is in the Old Testament. Amos is angry at God's people who are cheating the poor. Let's listen to his words.

(Put up the sign "Book of the Prophet Amos" on the lectern.)

SONG LEADER "Neighbors" *(Hi God III)*

GOSPEL

Luke 16:10-13

LESSON

(Children are asked to come up and sit on the floor.)

PRESENTER Jesus just said, "No servant can serve two masters. He will hate one and love the other." Do you know what Jesus means? Are we servants? Who is the Master?

I know a story about a boy named Jonathan that will shed a little light on this gospel message.

(Read "Jonathan's Gift" on the following pages. Presenter narrates as the appropriate picture transparencies are shown with an overhead projector, or drawn enlargements are placed on an easel. A flute melody is played at appropriate intervals as marked on the story with an *.)

JONATHAN'S GIFT
by Bernice Stadler

Illustrated by Deirdre Foley-DeVilbiss

Little Jonathan loved music. His most prized possession was an old but shiny flute given to him by his grandfather. On this flute he could play such happy notes that sounded like birds singing, * or low mellow sounds of a slow-moving brook. * Often on a summer's evening you could hear the sweet melody of Jonathan's flute floating down the streets of the village. *

"It is a gift you have, Jonathan," his grandfather would say, "a gift from God. Be sure to use this gift to serve him well."

Little Jonathan loved nothing more than to play his flute for his friends. He saw that it made them happy, even comforted them at times. And often when Jonathan was alone he would play a special melody to God praising and thanking God. The village was truly blessed with Jonathan's gift.

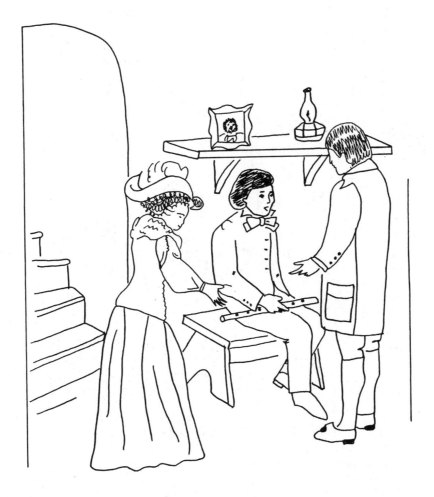

As the years passed, Jonathan grew to a young man and his friends would ask him what work he was to do when he became a man. He answered quickly, "I want to make others happy with my music." "You want to be a musician," they asked incredulously! "You can't make much money doing that." "I don't need much money. I live pretty simply,", Jonathan explained. "You want to get married some day, don't you?" "Who would want to marry you if you don't earn enough money?" "Don't you want the villagers to look up to you?" "How can you afford a home?" "Be practical, Jonathan!"

Their words worried Jonathan. He didn't want to appear foolish in the villagers eyes. So he followed the advice of his friends and began to find ways of earning money. Eventually he began a business and worked long hours, planning, organizing, and calculating. Because of his preoccupation and fatigue his precious flute was left on a shelf—no music was made.

In time, Jonathan earned plenty of money and, yes, he supported a wife and children. The villagers respected him as a responsible businessman and yet Jonathan was not happy. Something in his life was missing.

Alone in his room one evening, Jonathan absent-mindedly stared out his window. Feeling the familiar sadness creep over him, he went to busy himself at his desk when his eyes fell upon his old flute, half-hidden by a ledger in the bookcase. Retrieving the instrument, dusting it off with his shirt-tail, Jonathan returned to his chair. Thoughts of his grandfather and his younger days in the village flooded his memories.

Lifting his flute to his lips, Jonathan began to play a soft, sorrowful sound that opened his heart.* He closed his eyes and years of missed melodies tumbled from his grandfather's flute.*

When he finished, he noticed his wife standing by his shoulder and his children sitting on the floor in front of him. Wide-eyed, his son Paul exclaimed, "Papa, you have a wonderful gift? Why didn't you tell us?"

With a new-found peace filling his heart, he answered, "Yes, I have been given a gift. And I had forgotten to serve the one who gave it."

The End

What was Jonathan's gift? *(response. Children may say the "flute from his grandfather." The gift is the ability to make music on the flute, the gift of making others happy.)* Jonathan's grandfather told him to serve God well. Did he? *(response)* For a while he did but then he forgot didn't he? His friends told him that he made to make lots of money and then he would be important. Did he become important? Yes, he did, but was he happy? No, something was missing. What was it? *(response)* His music and serving God with it!

Do you know that we are to serve God? Yes, we are! He is the one master that Jesus speaks of in the gospel. We are to do what he wants us to do. Many times we forget this. Sometimes "false masters" like "Mr. Money" *(holding up cardboard prop)* or "Mr. Important" *(holding up cardboard prop)* come into our lives and say, "Follow me, and I will make you happy." And sometimes we believe them and follow them for a while.

Jesus warns us that there cannot be two masters in our lives only God. And, we are to use the gifts God has given us to serve God by serving our brothers and sisters.

We have a paper flute for each of you. On the flute is this prayer, "God our Father, you have given me the gift of _____. *(Think about something your have or you like to do.)* I will use this gift to serve you well." Amen.

You may all return to your seats now.

(The following is an optional teacher-blessing ceremony. It could be used if you are honoring your religious education teachers.)

PRESENTER There are some special people here today that serve their brothers and sisters by teaching . We are going to call them up here and give them our blessing.
Now, children, please stand and face the teachers. We are going to give them our blessing. Please raise both of your arms up like this. *(both arms raised up, palms facing teachers)* Now repeat each line after me:

("The Blessing Song" (Hi God II) may be sung or recited line by line.)

Thank you. You will be given a flute with a teacher's name on it. Will you promise to serve God and them by praying for that teacher each night? If you promise, please answer "I do."

(*response*) And now I ask the rest of the congregation, "Do you also make the same promise to serve God and to pray for these teachers?" We do!

You may all return to your seats.

COMMUNAL PRAYER

PRAYER LEADER Let us respond "Lord, hear our prayer."

Lord remember the teachers who are here with us today. They serve you with their gifts. Help them to grow in faith so that the children they teach may grow in faith and love of God. We pray to the Lord ... Lord, hear our prayer.

Lord, help us as a community to be less concerned with being wealthy and acquiring material goods. We pray to the Lord ... Lord, hear our prayer.

Lord, help us to be generous with our time and talents so that we can do the work for which you have called us. We pray to the Lord ... Lord, hear our prayer.

SONG LEADER "A Gift From Your Children" (*Hi God III*)

THANKS, GOD!

(TWENTY-EIGHTH SUNDAY OF THE YEAR—Fall)

2 Kings 5:14-17   2 Timothy 2:8-13   Luke 17:11-19

THEME   We want to be grateful children of God

PROPS
1. A picture of a large gift box hung on a wall or placed on an easel. This picture will be written on during the lesson.
2. Old sheets torn into strip bandages to be tied on each child's head or arm as they enter the celebration area.
3. Paper bells attached to yarn as necklaces to be distributed to each child before the celebration
4. 1 cow bell placed on the lectern
5. 1 bow placed on the lectern
6. 2 microphones in stands
7. Picture of a leper, if available

PERSONNEL
1. Presenter
2. Song Leader
3. Prayer Leader
4. Reader
5. Two children to read the opening meditation.
6. Jesus, 2 apostles, 2 lepers (older children)
7. Adult Helper

GREETING

PRESENTER   Welcome. What is our response to all of God's blessings? Are we a thankful people, a grateful people? The Scripture stories ask that question.

OPENING MEDITATION

CHILD 1   Mom says I should write thank you notes for my birthday gifts. I don't feel like it. Why should I anyway? I didn't ask for the gifts and some of them are really dumb, like the sweater from my aunt.

CHILD 2   Sure it's neat to receive gifts. Everyone likes getting gifts.

Grandma and Grandpa know I appreciate the money they send me for my birthday, don't they?

CHILD 1   Dad thinks I take people for granted, including him. I know he works hard all day. I know Mom works, too, so I can have nice school clothes and other things. Parents are suppose to do that, aren't they?

CHILD 2   Somehow I never find the time or the right words to tell Mom or Dad that I love them. They know I have a lot on my mind with other things. Besides they don't have to hear me say it, do they?

PRESENTER   Heavenly Father, take our careless self-centered hearts and change them into Spirit-filled hearts of thanksgiving. Amen.

FIRST READING

READER   2 Kings 5:14-17

SONG LEADER   "Receive Our Prayer" (*Hi God III*)

PRE-GOSPEL COMMENT

PRESENTER   Today the children are invited up into the sanctuary to help us act out the gospel. Before you sit down, please put one of these bells around your neck.

Do you know why you have these bandages today? You are all actors in our gospel. You will be playing the part of the lepers.

The reading that you have just heard and our gospel both talk about "lepers," people having leprosy. Can you say that word, "leprosy." (*Describe this disease a bit.*) It's a terrible disease that's been around since ancient times. It damages skin with bumps and open sores; there is loss of feeling in the toes and fingers. Sometimes fingers, hands, and feet can be lost. Blindness can occur and eventually death. (*Show a picture of a leper, if available.*) There is a medicine today to help the disease. There is hardly any leprosy in the United States, but people have always been terrified of catching this disease.

In the time of Jesus, lepers were the "outcasts," the feared people, the "untouchables." They were not allowed to sell or buy in the market-place. They could not worship in the church. They could not even talk or come near to the "normal" people. They even had to wear a noisemaker like this bell, like the bells around your necks, to call out to people to warn them that they were there. They would yell, "Unclean, unclean!" *(ring bell to demonstrate and yell out "Unclean, unclean!")* Since no one would hire them, they had to beg for their food. If you should happen to touch a leper by mistake, the law said you had to wait for a long time and then show yourself to the priest before you would be considered clean again.

So, this is the setting that Jesus walked into in today's gospel. We will tell our gospel as a play. Listen carefully. _____ *(adult helpers' names)* will tell you your parts.

(Adult helpers, Jesus, apostles, and lepers I and II need to be familiar with the script and practice before this celebration. One microphone is up stage, one rear stage.)

GOSPEL DRAMATIZATION

(Presenter narrates the gospel, with the Apostle and Leper interjecting side comments.)

PRESENTER   Jesus and his apostles were on their way to Jerusalem. They traveled along the border between Samaria and Galilee. As he was entering a village, ten lepers met him.

(As the priest says this, Jesus and his apostle slowly walk into the sanctuary and stop.)

APOSTLE   *(pointing to the lepers while looking fearful)* "Look, Jesus! Over there! Lepers!"

ADULT HELPERS   *(to the children)* Here comes Jesus. Now look up at Jesus and hold out your right hand like this and say all together, "Jesus, Master, take pity on us!" *(repeat it with the kids)*. Now hold both hands out and say it again: "Jesus, Master, take pity on us!"

JESUS   *(Walks over and touch the lepers kindly on the head or hand.)*

APOSTLES   *(Looks on in awe. Pointing at what Jesus is doing and talking to themselves.)*

PRESENTER   When Jesus saw them, he said to the lepers, "Go and show yourself to the priests."

JESUS   (*Points out to congregation and then walks back to the apostles and sits with them.*)

ADULT HELPERS (*to the children*) Pretend the priests are people sitting out in the congregation. Turn to them.

PRESENTER   After they were on their way to the priests they looked at their hands and feet and they realized that they were now clean.

LEPER 1   (*at microphone*) "Look at my hands! My skin is clear!" (*He takes off his bandages and looks joyful.*)

LEPER 2   "We're clean! We're clean! Take off your bandages my brothers and sisters. Wait until the priest sees us!" (*Takes off bandages, jumps for joy.*)

ADULT HELPERS (*to the children.*) Take off your bandages now. You are cured. Sit down.

LEPER 1   (*turning toward Jesus*) "Thank you, Jesus! Thank you, Jesus. Praise the Lord!" (*Starts to walk toward Jesus.*)

APOSTLE   (*looking nervous*) "Jesus, that leper is coming toward us. Watch out!"

LEPER 1   (*throwing himself at Jesus' feet*) "I'm clean. Thank you, Jesus."

APOSTLE   "He's clean! He's cured!"

PRESENTER   Jesus then asked the man, "Were not all made clean? The others—where are they?" It seems that no one has come back to give thanks to God except this foreigner.

APOSTLE   (*looking around*) "Jesus, they're all gone, not a sign of any of them."

PRESENTER   Jesus then said, "Stand up and go with God."

JESUS   (*helping the cured leper to his feet*) "Your faith has saved you." (*Jesus, apostles, and cured leper walk off together.*)

PRESENTER   This is the gospel of the Lord.

LESSON

PRESENTER What did the rest of the lepers forget to do in this Gospel? (*response*) Yes, to thank Jesus! Can you believe it! How ungrateful can they be? They were healed of the dreadful disease, but forgot to say thanks.

We're a bit like that, aren't we? We take lots of things for granted. God has given us so much. How good it is to say thank you.

Let's mention some of the gifts we want to thank God for right now. Lets write them on our paper gift box.

(Ask the children to write or the presenter may do the writing. Give them a marker. Ask the adults for suggestions too. After enough time—don't hurry this—tape the bow which is on the lectern on top of the paper "gift.")

PRESENTER Let us all say together, "Thank you, God." We will use sign language with our "thank you" (*Right hand fingers touch chin and arm draws out and up.*) So, repeat after me (*demonstrates*) "Thank you, God."

Your warning bells, children, can be changed into "thank you notes" like this. (*demonstrates by folding bell lengthwise, making a little card.*) Good! Take them to your supper table today and write a special "Thank you" to God from your family. That would make a beautiful prayer.

COMMUNAL PRAYER

PRAYER LEADER The response today is "Lord, hear our prayer."

Help us learn to be generous, generous with our money, our time, with our patience, we pray to the Lord... Lord, hear our prayer.
Help us be compassionate and helpful to those who are ill, especially those who have long-term illnesses, we pray ... Lord, hear our prayer.
Help us be sensitive to those schoolmates and neighborhood children who feel left out, we pray... Lord, hear our prayer.

SONG LEADER "Thank You Lord" (*Hi God I*)

KEEP PRAYING!

(TWENTY-NINTH SUNDAY OF THE YEAR—Fall)

Exodus 17:8-13   2 Timothy 3:14-4:2   Luke 18:1-8

THEME
: Persistence in prayer; no problem is hopeless

PROPS
: 1. A large picture of praying hands hung in a prominent place.
: 2. Card table and chair set up in worship space with a microphone beside the table. This will be used for the gospel.
: 3. 3 signs saying "Day 1," "Day 2," and "Week 3"
: 4. A choir robe for Judge to use during the gospel. Also a 9"x11" paper scroll.
: 5. 4 large signs: "Peace," "Sickness," "Hunger," and "Family Problems" attached to poles. Stands to hold these signs.
: 6. A picture of St. Augustine drawn on rolled paper approximately 4' long. Use an opaque projector to enlarge a small picture from a holy card or a book about saints.
: 7. A microphone set up in the front center of the worship space. This will be used for children with speaking parts.
: 8. Holy cards of saints to be passed out after the lesson.
: 9. A sign that says "Communal Prayer."

PERSONNEL
: 1. Presenter
: 2. Prayer Leader
: 3. Song Leader
: 4. Reader
: 5. 3 students to pantomime parts of judge, widow, and time-card holder in gospel
: 6. Student to be St. Monica during the lesson. She should dress in a long skirt and scarf
: 7. 4 Students to display signs and comment on these signs during the lesson.

GREETING

PRESENTER
: Good morning. The Scriptures today remind us that we are to pray with confidence, not with fear or doubt, but with confidence.

Let us pause with this thought for a moment ... Do I trust in God, my Father?

OPENING PRAYER

PRAYER LEADER Heavenly Father, you are a wonderful father to us! You have given us everything we need. You care about our troubles and our sorrows. Thank you for giving us Jesus to be with us always. Amen.

FIRST READING

READER The first reading is from Exodus (17:8-13). Exodus is in the Old Testament.

SONG LEADER "Our God Is a God of Love" (*Hi God I*)

PRE-GOSPEL COMMENT

PRESENTER Before we proclaim our gospel, the children are invited to come up and sit on the floor.

GOSPEL DRAMATIZATION

(The Presenter narrates the gospel. The widow inserts side comments. A student dressed in a black choir robe sits at a card table in the center of the worship space reading a newspaper with a loafing attitude.)

PRESENTER A reading from the holy gospel according to Luke.

Jesus told his disciples a parable on the necessity of always praying and not losing heart:

Once there was a judge in a certain city who respected neither God nor people. A widow in that city kept coming to him.

(Widow walks in, stands at the microphone near the judge. Another student stands to the right of the worship space with a sign, "Day 1".)

PRESENTER She would say to the judge:

WIDOW "I want justice from you against my enemy!"

PRESENTER   For a long time he refused.

(The Judge waves her away. The widow leaves, dejected. Sign holder changes sign to "Day 2." The widow walks to the microphone again.)

WIDOW   "Have you settled my case yet, Judge?"

(The Judge gets up pats her condescendingly on the back and shows her out. He sits again. Sign holder shows the third sign, "Week 3." The widow returns to the microphone.)

WIDOW   "Judge, you haven't forgotten me, have you?"

(The Judge acts exasperated and sends the woman out. He sits down, folds arms, then puts hand under his chin.)

PRESENTER   But at last he said to himself, "Maybe I have neither fear of God nor respect for man, but since she keeps pestering me, I must give this widow her just rights or she will persist in coming and worry me to death."

(During this narration, the Judge "tears his hair" in frustration. He then scribbles on a piece of paper, rolls it and walks to edge of the worship space. He beckons for the widow and hands her the scroll. She turns and leaves. The judge follows, shaking his head.)

PRESENTER   And the Lord said, "You notice what the unjust judge has to say? Now, will not God see justice done to his chosen ones who call out to him day and night? Will God delay long over them, do you suppose? I promise you he will see justice done to them, and done speedily! But when the son of man comes, will he find any faith on earth?"

This is the gospel of the Lord!

LESSON

PRESENTER   Children, have you ever felt like the woman in today's gospel? Needing something and having to ask over and over to get it? *(responses)*

MONICA   *(Walks in on cue.)* I can surely identify with that widow. *(nod-*

ding to the presenter and then to the children) Hello, _____. Hello, children. We have not met, but I'm sure you have heard of me. I'm St. Monica. I lived a long, long time ago.

PRESENTER   St Monica. Yes, we know of you. You're the mother of St. Augustine, one of the early church's finest teachers. As a matter of fact, I have a picture of St. Augustine right here. *(Holds up picture for all to see.)*

MONICA   Yes indeed! That's Augustine, but he didn't always look like that! I'm sad to say that for a long time my son's life was a mess. He was so very smart in school, but all he cared about was partying, drinking, wasting his time.

PRESENTER   You must have been upset. Did you talk to him, advise him?

MONICA   I talked to him until I was blue in the face! But I also talked to someone who would listen—God.

PRESENTER   And then Augustine changed, right?

MONICA   Yes he changed, but only after 18 years of praying! I never gave up. Just like that widow with the judge, I kept asking even though sometimes I felt it was a hopeless cause. *(talking to the children and the congregation)* That's why I'm here today, to urge you to never stop praying for your needs.

PRESENTER   Thank you for coming, St. Monica. *(She sits down.)* Children, each time we have a celebration, we ask for God's help in prayer we call *(holds up sign)* "Communal Prayer." Sometimes we ask God's help over and over again for certain things. Can you remember some of those needs we keep asking for? *(checks for responses, including the 4 children holding the signs.)*

CHILD 1   *(Brings up sign Peace)* We are always asking God for peace, especially world peace, so that wars will stop. *(Places sign in stand.)*

CHILD 2   *(Brings up sign World Hunger)* We usually pray for the hungry, especially in the countries that have drought, famine and poverty. *(Places sign in stand.)*

CHILD 3   (*Brings up sign The Sick*) We pray for the sick, those people who have cancer, AIDS, birth defects, mental illness. (*Places sign in stand.*)

CHILD 4   (*Brings up sign Family Problems.*) We also pray for family problems. Sometimes there is too much arguing and tension. (*Places sign in stand.*)

PRESENTER   These are just four of the needs we keep praying for. These problems have been with us a long time but like St. Monica we will not be discouraged. We'll keep asking God to show us the way to solve these problems. The Spirit will guide us.

MONICA   And children, not only can all of *you* pray, but you can also ask my friends in heaven to pray—we're part of your family too. We want to support you. I have some pictures and prayers of the saints here. I would like to give you all a picture. Would my helpers please help me hand these out. You may return to your seat after you get your picture.

COMMUNAL PRAYER

PRAYER LEADER   Heavenly Father, we have just mentioned the constant needs we ask you to fulfill. We seek an end to family problems, and world peace. It is with confidence that we ask and with assurance we wait. Amen.

SONG LEADER   "Receive Our Prayer" (*Hi God III*)

WORDS OF WISDOM

(THIRTY-THIRD SUNDAY OF THE YEAR—Fall)

Malachi 3:19-20   2 Thesalonians 3:7-12   Luke 21:5-19

THEME   God's holy word gives us the wisdom to bear and solve the world's brokenness

PROPS   1. A broken bicycle is on display. Its wheel and chain are off.

2. Three books covered with colored paper and labeled, 1) "Bicycle Repair," 2) "Building a Backyard Playhouse," 3) "The Complete Cookbook."

3. A world map that has been cut irregularly into 4 large sections and then fitted back into a whole is displayed on a flannel board. Signs indicating world troubles, such as Wars, Terrorism, Nuclear Accidents, Natural Disasters, and Crime are taped onto the flannel board underneath the segments of the world map. When the map is pulled apart, the signs are exposed.

4. 2 signs of advice given in today's gospel. "I have given you the words of Wisdom" and "By patient endurance you will save your lives."

5. A Bible on a stand in front of the pulpit with candle beside it.

6. Bible bookmarks and Bible dedication ceremony sheets to be passed out after the lesson.

PERSONNEL   1. Presenter

2. Prayer Leader

3. Song Leader

4. Reader

GREETING

PRESENTER   Good morning. There's a broken bicycle and some instruction manuals here in the sanctuary. Perhaps they're clues to today's Scripture message. Are things falling apart? Let us prepare ourselves to hear God's message.

OPENING PRAYER

PRAYER LEADER Heavenly Father, source of wisdom, we look to you to guide us. We are lost without you. Thank you for sending Jesus, your word, among us. Amen.

FIRST READING

READER Malachi 3:19-20

SONG LEADER "Remember Your Love and Care" (*CTWWS*)

GOSPEL

PRESENTER Luke 21:5-19

LESSON

PRESENTER Children, please come up and sit near this broken bicycle and our world map so that we can talk about the gospel we have just heard.

Let's take a look at this bike. What's wrong with it? (*response - wheel missing, the chain is off*) I really don't know too much about bikes. Let's see, which of these books do you think would help me fix this bike? (*Picks up each book.*) "The Complete Cookbook"?(*no*) "Building a Backyard Playhouse"? (*no*) How about "Bicycle Repair"? (*yes*) Right, you know where to look for good advice.

Let's take a look at our world map here. In many ways our world can be like our broken bike. We can say our world is often "torn apart" by:

(*At this time spread the map sections apart exposing the titles of troubles underneath. Do this one at a time, having the children read the title. Elaborate a bit on each one so they will understand the problem.*)

Wars: Ireland, Central America, Lebanon
Terrorism: bombing, kidnapping, hijacking
Nuclear Accidents: Chernobyl
Natural Disasters: floods, droughts, volcano eruptions, earthquakes
Crime: drugs, robbery, murder

These are big problems, aren't they? How do we fix our world? Is there a repair manual we can turn to? (*response*) A repair manual, like this one, no, but in a real sense there is a book we can turn to for good advice. It is this book. (*Holds up Bible*.) Do you know what it is called? (*response*) Yes, The Holy Bible. Jesus' words, and the Father's words are in this book. The wisdom about knowing God and living in this world with each other is in this book.

In our gospel today, Jesus talked about big troubles like these (*pointing at the easel*). He gave 2 important pieces of advice. (*putting up sign*) "I have given you the words of wisdom" and "By patient endurance you will save your lives." This means, Don't get all upset about your problems. God is with us.

How many of you have a Bible at home? (*show of hands*) Good! It's important to read it with your families so that God's wisdom may enter our minds and hearts, so that we can solve our world's brokenness.

Let's make a pledge and bless ourselves as we do every Sunday before the gospel is read. With your right thumb (*motion*) we are going to make a cross first on your forehead, then on our lips, and then our hearts. Now all please repeat after me. "May the wisdom of the word of God (*mark cross on Bible*) be in my mind + on my lips + and in my heart. + Amen."

We have a Bible dedication ceremony written for your families along with a book mark to place in your family Bible. Please sit down together with your family this week and pray this blessing.

My helpers will give you the bookmark as you return to your seats now.

COMMUNAL PRAYER

PRAYER LEADER   Please respond, "Lord, give us your wisdom."

Lord, help us to be conscious of your power to heal, let us pray ... Lord, give us your wisdom.

Lord, help us to make the world a better place in which to live, let us pray ... Lord, give us your wisdom.

Lord, help us to remember those in need and share our lives with them, let us pray ... Lord, give us your wisdom.

SONG LEADER   "Let Their Be Peace on Earth" (*Traditional*)

BIBLE DEDICATION CEREMONY

(Create a setting: Place your family bible in a prominent position in the living room along with a vase of flowers or plant and a candle in a holder.)

LEADER   *(lifting the Bible)* We gather here as a family to honor this holy book, the word of God.

PARENT   O Lord, through these writings you have shown yourself to us. You have chosen us to be your special people and you are our God.

CHILD   *(lighting the candle)* You have given us Jesus your Son. He is the light of the word. He is your living word among us.

LEADER   John 1:14

ALL   *(placing hand on Bible)* Lord God, may these writings give us a deep understanding of you and of ourselves. May it strengthen our love for you. May it lead us to active concern for all our brothers and sisters. We ask this through Jesus. Amen.